# HEART'S HUNGER

# Heart's Hunger

## Selected Poems

### Karen Press

2024 © Karen Press
All rights reserved

ISBN 978-1-928476-52-8
ebook ISBN 978-1-928476-53-5

Deep South, Makhanda, South Africa
contact@deepsouth.co.za
www.deepsouth.co.za

Distributed in South Africa by
Blue Weaver Marketing and Distribution
https://blueweaver.co.za

Distributed worldwide by
African Books Collective
PO Box 721, Oxford, OX1 9EN, UK
www.africanbookscollective.com/publishers/deep-south

Cover art: Lien Botha *Piero di Cosimo*
digital photographic deconstruction
from the *In Afterland* series, 2022

Cover design: JMS Design
Text design and layout: Liz Gowans
Proofreading: Danya Ristić-Schacherl

The author and publisher thank the University of KwaZulu-Natal Press
for their generous permission to use poems from *Echo Location: A Guide
to Sea Point for Residents and Visitors* (Gecko Poetry, UKZN Press, 1998)
and *The Little Museum of Working Life* (UKZN Press, 2004)

The author and publisher thank Carcanet Press
for their generous permission to use poems from *Home* (Carcanet, 2000),
*The Canary's Songbook* (Carcanet, 2005) and *Slowly, As If* (Carcanet, 2012)

# Contents

from *Bird Heart Stoning the Sea*

| | |
|---|---|
| This winter coming | 11 |
| Not forgetting | 13 |
| Krotoa's story | 14 |

from *Echo Location:*
*A Guide to Sea Point for Residents and Visitors*

| | |
|---|---|
| Prologue | 33 |
| Nineteenth-century gratitude | 34 |
| The first thirty-seven years | 35 |
| Glimpses of women in overalls | 36 |
| Tips for visitors | 38 |
| Causality and chance in love | 39 |
| Seaworthy | 42 |

from *The Little Museum of Working Life*

| | |
|---|---|
| Working life | 47 |
| Diorama: weekend work | 48 |
| Mostly through the eyes of a child | 49 |
| Pocket money | 50 |
| The room of watching | 51 |
| The room of how to | 53 |

from *Home*

| | |
|---|---|
| Heart's hunger | 59 |
| Needle work | 64 |
| I who live here, it is I | 65 |
| Dispossessed words | 68 |
| Leader | 70 |
| Reclaiming our land | 71 |
| Incarnate eternity | 72 |

Tiresias in the city of heroes     77

from *The Canary's Songbook*
- Broken bits of the past     87
- Knocking series     88
- Treasure trail     91
- Stones for my pockets     92
- Men wear the secret masks     93
- In Jakob's house     94
- Ox blood poisons the ground with longing     98
- Visiting home     99
- The personal assistant     100
- Redistributing it     101
- Oral tradition     102
- Flakes of the light falling     103
- Book     105
- Walking songs for Africans abroad     109
- Globalisation     115
- Aching     116
- Soft     118
- A certain history     119
- The canary's songbook     120

from *Slowly, As If*
- Cyrus Vance sat on my couch     123
- And all the time     125
- Monument to the South African Republic     130
- Eight frescoes from the lost palaces of Zanj     132
- Man series I     140
- The sad little poems     142
- Pasternak's shadow     143
- Love songs for Lake Como     145

| | |
|---|---|
| Over there | 147 |
| I saw you coming towards me | 153 |
| Elaine's garden | 161 |
| Tango for person and city | 167 |
| Deer on the freeway | 174 |
| Phendukani Silwani | 175 |
| Poem for which there was no title | 179 |
| *from* Folk dancing for beginners | 185 |
| *Arīb is Known: Six Songs in Search of a Singer* | 195 |

from *The Loving and Lovable City (May Not Yet Be Here): An Atlas of the Cape Peninsula*

| | |
|---|---|
| Songs for the tourist in Cape Town | 207 |
|    Booked tour | 207 |
|    Itinerary | 208 |
|    Gap year tourist | 209 |
|    Departure | 210 |
|    Once I travelled | 211 |
| Sites of interest | 212 |
|    Factreton | 212 |
|    Clifton | 213 |
|    Brackenfell | 214 |
|    Elfindale | 215 |
|    Muizenberg | 216 |
|    District Six c. 2020 | 217 |
|    The Castle of Good Hope | 218 |
| Unmapped | 219 |
| | |
| Source notes | 222 |

from *Bird Heart Stoning the Sea*

(1990)

## This Winter Coming

Walking in the thick rain
of this winter we have only just entered,
who is not frightened?

The sea is swollen, churning in broken waves
around the rocks, the sand is sinking away
the seagulls will not land
under this sky, this shroud falling
who is not frightened?

In every part of the city, sad women climbing onto buses,
dogs barking in the street, and the children
in every doorway crying,
the world is so hungry, madam's house is clean
and the women return with slow steps
to the children, the street, the sky tolling like a black bell;
these women are a tide of sadness
they will drown the world,
who is not frightened?

On every corner men standing
old stumps in the rain, tombstones
engraved with open eyes
watching the bright cars full of sated faces
pass them, pass them, pass them,
who is not frightened?

Into the rain the children are running
thin as the barest twigs they kindle a fire
to fight the winter, their bare bodies
a raging fire of dead children

and the sky collapsing under centuries of rain
the wind like a mountain crying,
who is not frightened of this winter
coming upon us now?

## Not forgetting

Summer's coming, despite everything,
sit on the beach and think of your brother
in prison, remember your sister in the graveyard
spread out your towel and imagine
one thin line of sky painted behind bars and walls
cold as a black coffin, buy an ice-cream
for your brother, taste it with your sister's tongue
ride a wave for each of them, you must
live three times over now, not forgetting yourself.

## Krotoa's story

*Prologue*

the scouts came back and said
there are three ships in the bay, men everywhere
like beetles, digging, breaking stones, women also,
we did not go near the rivers

who are they who are they who are they who are they

we spoke with Doman, who has been watching them
he says they have come to live here
they are building a big place, a fort,
they have guns, said Doman, and seeds which they plant

women also?
women also
guns, and three ships
they are Dutch

what do they want what do they want what do they want

Doman says they have been here a long time
they send men up the coast
to see what is there
they do not shoot
but they count everything

why did Doman not come to tell us?
Doman has his own thoughts
he is not our enemy, but he is not our friend

around the fire, talking, until the stars faded

Oedasoa went to his compound, and the elders with him
something new has come into the world
something must go out from us, to meet it

1

I am Krotoa.

I am the daughter of Maqona.
My sister is the wife of the great Cochoqua chief, Oedasoa,
and in his kraal I, Krotoa,
spend my time with the women of his household.

When I am older I shall marry one of the sons of the rich men
among us. I have already chosen from them
two whose looks and actions I shall watch
as they grow older. Then the chief Oedasoa, my brother,
will arrange the wedding with the one who is bravest
and most handsome.

Now I learn the skills
of basket weaving, shaping pots and finding plants that heal.
My sister teaches me to plait my hair
and to make ornaments for my body from copper wire.

Walking alone through the bushes
I feel the sun turning my skin to gold
and the hot wind playing against my legs:
at such times I know how beautiful I am.

There are two kinds of people:
the ones who huddle over the ground
afraid that their fingers will drop off before the work is done,

and those who climb trees and cry out
to see how many birds they can put to flight.

I know I will not be satisfied
until I have frightened the black-winged hawk
off his perch in the high mountains.
Heitsi-Eibib will bless me, and keep me from danger.

\*

it was Oedasoa himself who came to call me,
my sister plaiting my hair in the sun
next to the old tree, and his shadow fell
over us suddenly so that we both jumped up
stood heads bowed before him
my sister spoke, what is it, my lord?
what can I do? and he, nothing, nGai,
it is Krotoa I have come to find
my face hot as fire, he has not done this before
pain dived into my sister's eyes and disappeared
Oedasoa took my hand, come, Krotoa,
I must explain something to you, something we want
you to do to help protect your people from the strangers

I went with him
I sat beside him on a stone
and he instructed me

afterwards I went out to the edge of the camp
and sat where a bush owl slept on a tree
but the sounds of the earth seemed to move away from me
like birds drawing back from a fresh kill
after a while there was silence

and though I fixed my eyes on the owl's claws
it was Oedasoa's voice that beat on my ears
until I couldn't see anything
couldn't hear anything

like a dry twig
fallen off a tree
I sat silently in the long grass

\*

who is this person Oedasoa has commanded
I have not met her before

who is this person who will go
and live among strangers
to learn their meaning?

her name is Krotoa, but I do not know her

\*

riding on a shining ox
high above the shoulders of the men
the long grass touching my feet
I am the chief's sister
everyone knows my mission
I am the young one, the clever one
sent to meet the strangers
I am the pointed spear
flung into the heart of the enemy
I will return over these grasses
trailing their secrets like the entrails

of the captured impala
I have been blessed by Heitsi-Eibib
I have been covered in the perfumed fat of the chief's pot
sitting in the sun I ride
into the heart of the enemy

2

the first time I saw them
the wind was as strong as always
in summer here, under a mountain of white clouds
all their tents had blown down
and as we rode towards them they stood ready to greet us
formally, as befits a meeting of chiefs
but the wind was blowing off their hats,
their jackets flapped, long spears kept knocking
at their legs, some of them were worrying
about things falling over where the tents were
they didn't know how to stand in the wind
could never keep their balance

(it was like that through all the seasons,
too hot, and their skin turned red and fell off
or raining till their boots filled up;
half of them were always sick,
they could not live the seasons of this country
but they stayed
in spite of everything, our weather and our gods
had no effect on them)

I went forward, but first Oedasoa went forward
as befits a chief, went forward on his red ox
and dismounted, stood with his shield beside him
and his spear planted in the ground

then their chief came towards him, a man
with feathers and a folded cloth on his head
came forward with his long brown hair curling
came forward and bowed, not very low
stood still, looking at Oedasoa
each of them spoke, then there was silence
they did not know each other's words

Autshomoa appeared, my own Autshomoa
brother of my mother's home, where had he been?
came to the chiefs, they spoke to him
and he gave their words one to the other
in a way that could be understood

I went to stand beside the ox
with my eyes I greeted Autshomoa
Oedasoa put his hand on my head
and gave me as a gift to the chief with long hair
Autshomoa repeated the giving, in strange words
the chief looked at me, and spoke
Autshomoa took me in our language for the chief
I walked past Oedasoa
I stood beside the tents blown down

3

In the night of that first day, I did not know what I was.
Prisoner?
Guest?
No one spoke to me. They showed me to a room. Dark, cold, like skins soaked in rain and forgotten. I stayed there until so long had passed that I seemed to have gone far away.

Then I thought, I must see whether I am free, went
out of the room, walked, following the smell of air
until I came out under the sky.

It was warm, but there was no one anywhere.

Standing outside the walls I looked at the stars, neck bent back
I imagined round me the fire where they were all sitting now, on
the other side of the mountain, the stories, songs, nGai next to
me, I cried, but silently in case this was not allowed. I did not
know what to do except go back inside and wait to be called.
I could not find my room, so I stayed in the open place between
the walls where they keep their animals. In the morning I woke
up, two men were standing laughing at me, I felt afraid. I stood
up and waited in front of them looking at the ground. When
they had stopped laughing they went to let out the animals,
I followed the cattle and sheep outside, no one stopping me.
There was one I recognised, a cow from Oedasoa's kraal, I used
to milk her. I could not stop myself from crying.

I could keep walking, would they stop me?
I could go back across the veld and over the mountain,
no one has talked to me, I could just blow away like a leaf
going back to its tree – then Autshomoa's eyes found me,
and tied me down to this place.

*

I learn Dutch.

I say 'Good morning', 'Thank you', 'My name is Eva'

I say 'Commander Jan van Riebeeck says'

these are the words I learn:

ox sheep dress table mevrouw hottentot mountain ship dutch
sea pearls because soon gold milk far exchange danger skins
man sick wine copper meat holland slave bed shoes bring god
one many bible elephant onions boundary promise

I say 'My name is Eva'

Commander Jan van Riebeeck taught me

Eva dress shoes
Eva room dark
Eva eyes
Eva mouth

Eva is the Dutch word for Krotoa

\*

who is Autshomoa? who is Doman? who is Oedasoa?
they ask me, the Council men in their dark cloths
who is the chief of your people? where do they live?
where are the hunting grounds for elephants?
where do the slaves go when they run away?

the Council men in their dark cloths ask me
and I try to find the right words for answers

Autshomoa is from my home, sirs, from my childhood,
                                                  he sang to me
and Doman is from another place
where the Chainouqua make war against us

Oedasoa is the greatest chief of us all, but Gogosoa
sets his people to take our animals, and Doman is against us,
he is from the other mountains where I lived, where
                                            Autshomoa was
before I went to Oedasoa, sirs, the elephants do not come
                                                      near us,
it is dangerous to hunt them, Doman is dangerous, sirs,
Oedasoa is the chief of us all, he sends you greetings,
he does not steal slaves, we do not know slaves

the Council men whip their dark cloths around them angrily,
they say, your Autshomoa steals our sheep,
he is in league with Doman against us
and I say, no sirs, no, no, sirs, Autshomoa does not steal,
the sheep are from Oedasoa, our chief, a gift
                                    for your Commander,
it is Doman who is against you, and against Oedasoa,
he wants war against us all,
it is his people who take the slaves

but I cannot explain and I cry, I think Oedasoa would
                                                  be angry,
but the Commander comes forward and says, thank you Eva,
he leads me gently away from the room and the Council men

\*

on a day nGonnomoa came to me
came from home, all the way
with buchu leaves for perfume from nGai, with greetings
from everyone and from Oedasoa? no, Oedasoa said
                                       nothing for you,
only we need to know more about what is happening here

you must tell me everything

nGonnomoa came, on his way to greet the Commander
and said show me the inside
of your room
I took him there
fearful of being seen
he was afraid in the small dark space
I could see how he tried
not to touch the walls
he stood with one foot in the doorway
but his hand was on my back
and I drew him in
his hand the warmest thing in that cold place
I made him come to my bed
I made him pull off me the thick dress
and when I saw our two bodies
shining like fire in that dark
I cried and cried to be out in the sunlight
then he pierced me and I clung to his legs
the smell of his skin made me drunk
when I opened my eyes he was gone
in the darkness I covered myself with the slave girl's dress

*

the Commander calls me
there are visitors
Doman is there nGonnomoa is there
the Commander asks me to interpret
I smile at him
his hand is on my shoulder
Doman stares at me

nGonnomoa stares at me
I tell the visitors more cattle are needed
I tell the Commander one cow will be brought
I tell the visitors that is not enough
I tell the Commander more may be brought after the rains
I tell the visitors there is brandy and tobacco for them outside
I tell the Commander the visitors thank him
the Commander's hand is on my shoulder
Doman and nGonnomoa leave
me there

outside the fort they were laughing
and drinking the brandy
when I came to sit with them they were silent

Doman says
whose side are you on, Krotoa?

I say
I am where you put me

4

after many seasons I went home
in the spring, back to my people, I said goodbye
to the Commander, to the Dutch Council,
they gave me presents for my services,
I promised them I would remember their interests
at home, and I left them

but in the autumn I returned

(my home, my path over the mountains,
and this chair of dark wood in the office

where I have sat watching the Commander,
soft hair bending over me, gentle hands
in this dark cave, my flowers, my yellow birds
calling me, I am coming to you!)

*

nGai was sick, dying, but I came
and they had to listen to me:
Heitsi-Eibib has brought sickness among you
because you would not tell the Commander
where to find the secret nest of pearls and gold,
but I will ask Jesus to make you better, nGai,
Jesus is the Son of God, God is father
to us all, the Commander taught me that,
he has been good to us, nGai,
he would not let you die

and they praised me greatly for the things I had learnt
among the Dutch
and nGai lived
and they all began to pray to God, Oedasoa ordered it
I taught them how

in the autumn I returned to the fort
to learn more of the Dutch, and their ways
Oedasoa ordered it

*

I've learnt something now
I tell them what they want to hear
and they love me for it

don't be angry with me, Oedasoa,
this way they trust me:
I am treated like a Dutch lady, now

and Doman, who complains, is sly
the Commander does not trust him
and nor should you, Oedasoa,
he plots against us all
trust me

\*

but they have put Autshomoa away
on the prison island, my own uncle, and I beg
the Commander, I will do anything
and the Commander agrees to free him
why, I can't be sure, I am frightened
I try to tell them everything, but they are talking without me

and now it is Doman
they call, I am left
free all day to wander where I will
what is happening?

\*

nGai is dead, oh, and I am far away
they will do the slow dance
nGai, nGai, you are dead
and I am far away

\*

and no message came from Oedasoa
no word ever from the women mourning
for nGai, my sister

when the men come with the animals to the fort
they do not ask for me, I am forgotten

I am forgotten, the Commander has gone away
alone here, I keep to my room
or talk to the sailors in the harbour

those who live on ships are friendly
towards a stranded creature

\*

now, look!
I am a lady, with a house, and silver wedding plate
from the Council, I have a husband
a ship's surgeon, an important man

I am a wife
I am Mevrouw van Meerhoff
he will go on missions for the Council
he will take me with him everywhere
husband
wife

Oedasoa, did they ever tell you
what a fine house I live in?

5

no word came for me from Oedasoa, ever

and so I stayed among those people
became a Dutch wife, learned
to speak in long Dutch sentences,
became a widow, standing like a wild buck
in the yard of the foreigners

they would not take me in, hottentot woman
nor would they let me run away, they broke my legs

mine are the crippled footprints
worn into the rocks along the harbour wall

the beginning was an exploding sun
I ran dancing into the fire
the end unravelled like an old root,
dry with sorrow, lasting forever


*Epilogue*

I am looking for one bird –
a bird from the flock of tall lagoon-dwellers
that I watched quietly digging for fish
in the waters of my childhood –
one who will listen to me
and then tell my story to one other
who in turn will pass it on
along the edges of the lagoon
up and down the coast these ships follow
forever, let it lodge between the stones of every beach

where my own tears have carried on the waves
to moor themselves:

Krotoa became Eva
and then became again
Krotoa

died at the Cape, 29th July 1674
and is remembered

from *Echo Location:*
*A Guide to Sea Point for Residents and Visitors*

(1998)

## Prologue

Mesmerised
by a bead on a string
(and the string is a net
and the net falls over us
and) we lie there like silver fish
staring entranced at the smiling sky
that smells like sea, and it's so blue we forget
we're not breathing

in this tideless bowl of bliss,
dreamstruck

in the present tense that never leaves
the shadow of the old mantis
lifting the strings of the bikini top
in his slow claws, pulling them loose:

fresh bread of all countries rises like angels
in clouds of cinnamon sugar and olive oil,
hearts discover their many mouths sipping
the small boys in doorways, the tanned girls on corners,
and framed by driftwood limbs

the day swells like a downy peach
over whose sweet flesh a child rides a tricycle

gleefully round and round, spreading
the gold urine of an enormous dog

in spirals, wider and wider,
entranced by its sour shimmer.

## Nineteenth-Century Gratitude

Sea captains come to anchor here,
unloading fattened dreams of dark barbarity,
shaking the crumbs of insignificance from their beards.

Their wives unearth the tranquil soil,
plant children, servants and the pincers of God's charity.
Leopards and forests are turned away.

The lion's rump, bought from a guttural horseman,
is sliced into parlour views and roses.
Natives are covered with cloth and kept moving.

Municipal power fills each tobacco pouch.
The sea seems to have learnt placidity.
Fog rises only at night, pacing the sand in silence.

Ships founder visibly on the rocks.
The captains frown at the drowning cries
their grandchildren collect in candy-striped sunhats.

Should they be thanking someone?
The wind blows in from Gallows Hill,
reminding them to relax.

Dark hands wheel their Bath chairs along.
Their wives exchange recipes for wreaths.
The sun peels their skin.

## The First Thirty-Seven Years

We were just camping out.
I put up a wall
and my mother bought carpets.
There was a door for the sea.

My father stood dropping anchor
year by year. I watched him lowering the rope,
he was swaying with a faraway look
and he said he loved me, lowering the rope.

My brother kicked a ball around a lot
and I was reading. I never knew
he broke his heart young.
I buried mine in a wave.

My father died. My mother went home.
My brother was away somewhere, walking.
I moved to the other side of the wall,
just camping out.

The sea could come in my sleep, or the wind.
I've no rope, my father left no rope.

## Glimpses of women in overalls

*live-in*

tin gives you no time, only
everything too hot, the taste of your own burnt tongue
immediately going cold, coagulation of fat on the palate

they say china holds the warmth,
allowing incredible flavours to seep like perfume
through the soft, moist cells that glow with pleasure
behind closed lips

*off duty*

like children, fearing any moment
the door bursting open:
why did you
where is my
who said you

*one of the family*

shadow
moving quietly along the world's outline
sharpening the brilliance of its whirling blades
the keys, the voices, dancing, dust-free

*yet somehow a stranger*

bridge on heavy legs,
the strong right arm supporting
untold numbers of children and their parents,

maltese poodles, hot water cylinders, supermarkets, lavatories
the other jointed like a cracked wing,

reaching into the mist, as far as the eye can see
along its length pigeons building nest after nest,
the soft-throated rumbling of their incomprehensible songs
barely audible

## Tips for visitors

Eat slowly and sip water frequently.
Close envelopes with extra glue.
Everything warms up.
The thin small angular men with low-slung pants are
                              the dangerous ones.
You need never be satisfied with yesterday's bread.
Ask at any corner café for doctors, dentists, vets,
physiotherapists, manicurists, hairdressers, dieticians or
                    psychologists in your vicinity.
Carry your keys in a separate pocket.
The mist is clean and good for your skin.
Small bushes at ground level contain rats.
Don't visit the library if you're in a hurry.
There are tiny green parks on many corners.
People shouting are not calling you.
Fresh water is available in all public toilets.
Never sit alone in a park.
All pharmacies sell chocolates.
Halaal food is safer.
On hot evenings big things fly through windows.
Count your change.

## Causality and chance in love

*Chapter 1*

His parents
and my parents
caused it all.

That's not true. God, laughing as he turned the page.

Two atoms coughed out
by time's collapsing star.

Libra ascending straight into Scorpio
through Sharpeville, Robben Island and Mowbray.
Arriving in Sea Point
when the law was repealed.

Now we are possible.
Necessary and sufficient conditions.

This happy world that fills our arms.

*Chapter 2*

Robben Island was more useful
than the little Swiss chalet
with the man and the lady
swinging in and out unreliably
or stuck; the mercury still as a dead ant.

| IF YOU SEE | IT WILL BE |
|---|---|
| the clear outline of the island | rain is on the way, and winter winds |
| a smudge of land in a brown haze | there is dangerous smog in the air |
| a shimmering blue blur | there will be long and windless heat |

'The healthy colony of penguins
is Robben Island's pride and joy.'

'I remember the first time all of us heard children's voices in the quarry. It was as though we had suddenly been struck by lightning. We all stood dead still, and every one of us was waiting for the moment when we would glimpse that child. And of course it wasn't allowed. The warders quickly went and made sure that we didn't actually see the kids. Just those lone voices – the one occasion in ten years that I actually heard the voice of a child.'

*Chapter 3*

Mist rising on the winter waves
swathed your quarried words in veils
and blew them in to fill my chest with sleeplessness.

I watched the kelp arms of sea creatures reaching
                                        through the swell.
You caught the glint of closed windows on the sunlit hills.

Only the wind passing across your lips
and then across my lips, preoccupied with its cargo of rain,
could have imagined us both in the same breath.

*Chapter 4*

We two waltzing strangely across sand bearing us
tideward, looking over each other's shoulders

at our futures, their lightless eternities
radiating power. Space is curved. We will meet each other

again and again in our pasts that call themselves home,
a little distance from the sunset come to fetch us.

This laughing history that fills our arms.

## Seaworthy

Not retreating
from your cuts and your sores
plastered over,
from your caverns
where rats buy endless rounds of drinks,
from your weeping pavements
and your salt glare,
not shunning the burnt skin
you burnish like shields
and your acid kisses,
not hiding here in my green heart
I am rising,
with my ropes of hunger and my bare feet
I am coming out
to gird you,
your northwest memory
and your southeast curses,
your holds full of golden bones and baby hair,
your raw hull torn through the soil
and filled with seeds,
I am casting my nets
over your glass sails with their arrogant wings,
over your moontrapped mast
and the diamonds stashed in your wicked crow's nest:
holding all your ends together
drawing you close to me,
welding you to my childhood shoulders,
lifting you through the first swell

I breast the ocean waiting for us, sure
of your weathered shadow that will be my raft,
and my hand-knotted song, your sounding line:
now we are sailing into the deep century rising under us,
not sinking.

from *The Little Museum of Working Life*

(2004)

## Working life

Working life began with apples falling from trees and a cow,
then came babies and lots of washing, arrows, horses, guns,
ways of stuffing a chicken and beaten metal
all over the world

and then wage labour,
grown-ups and children climbing into morning machines
and falling out of them at night without speaking, thin
bundles of hunger tied up with worries.

When the machines stop working life ends
except for the sea still trying to help,
colouring its undrinkable water every blue and green
for the broken shells to remember:
river blues and harvest greens.

## Diorama: weekend work

Four children massaging their father's body
on a Saturday afternoon.

Forehead neck fingers feet
feet fingers neck forehead.

Look it's swollen
I can wobble this bone
smooth the creases
rub till it's hot, it goes soft.

Forty fingers washing him
with their dusty whispers.

He floats into sleep on their giggling departure,
coins in the back yard dropping into a bottle.

## Mostly through the eyes of a child

Mostly through the eyes of a child
working life is so big,
full of worry and machines.
Be quiet daddy's tired.

Mostly through the eyes of a child
don't touch anything.
Say good morning to Mrs Boss.
I'll be home late.

Mostly through the eyes of a child
fireman vet pilot dancer.
What does your mom do?
Why doesn't your dad work?

If the boss was kind there'd be money.
No one at home would shout.
Dad would love me better.
Mom would be beautiful and I'd get good marks
and be everyone's favourite.

## Pocket money

apricot balls
orange red
marshmallow fish
pink white yellow
stale powdery
cracked skin like my mom's feet
liquorice twists
soft on Monday hard on Thursday
suck before you chew
brown lips black tongue
niknaks turn your fingers orange
oily crumbs all over your chin
I'll swop you I'll swop you
your dad drinks meths
your mom cleans bogs
give me your fish I'll give you my apricot
look at your tongue
look at yours

## The Room of Watching

window for watching
the maids and the caretaker waste time

corner from which you can watch
the machinist's hands letting cloth fall into her bag

glass door for watching
the dough rise in the tin

camera that shows
the cows turning back from the blades

gangway for counting
the heads of the belt operators

screen for showing
the planes moving through each other's paths

lens for watching
the sperm burrow into the egg

fence for watching
the wheat grow

rooftop for watching
your sister walk home across the dangerous field

hole for watching
the builders dig the foundations of the tower

crow's nest for watching
the land let go of you

glass wall for watching
a baby breathe

screen for watching
the heart weaken

spy hole for watching
the prisoner think

# THE ROOM OF HOW TO

*All types of work fall into one of the categories counting, cleaning, making, carrying.*
— *Codex of Working Life*

Stepping carefully
around and between the pieces of the bus
start by counting how many school bags,
then how many whole bodies,
how many separated legs divide by two,
how many hair ribbons and dirty handkerchiefs,
how many fingers,
how many left feet,
then map these onto
the number of empty seats flung wide
over the road and the surrounding veld,
how many of them still sticky
with jam and spilled cooldrinks.

\*


Use water on the fingers and the cheeks
a soft brush to lift beetles and thorns out of the hair
soap for the torn clothes and for the fresh clothes
                    to bury them in
a firm brush for the grit under the nails
tweezers for the glass splinters
tape to lift off the tar
witch hazel to clean the blood away
but for the bruises nothing, they are the dead hearts' ghosts,
they will stay there.

\*

They loved green apples
so make the coffins from apple wood, cut down all the trees
they climbed and shook laughing
to bounce apples into skirts and school bags.

And cut down the plum tree they teased for its blossoms,
make the coffin lids from plum wood stained with petals.

The nails must be taken from the walls of bedrooms
where they held up posters of heroes
and kept shoes safe from puppies.
Take out all the nails.

Melt down their CDs and radios, their earrings
                              and house keys,
and forge the grey lump into ugly handles
that will hurt the hands of the pallbearers,
make them cut deep and leave scars
the length of children's screams.

\*

Carry them as if they were sleeping snakes
as if they were rocks under which scorpions are waking up
as if they were owls spewing curses
as if they were phials of acid spilling onto your skin.

Carry them slowly, so slowly that you will never reach
the place where you can put them down,
a dry place with deep holes surrounded by earth

where mothers and fathers sway like crows
where a priest beckons you with his purple scarf.

Carry them like children on a holiday bus
looking back at their waving friends
looking up at the oncoming taxi,
running backwards inside the bus moving forward
                            and screaming uselessly
inside the bus moving forward.

Carry them backwards, they are not finished living yet
keep carrying them.

from *Home*

(2000)

# HEART'S HUNGER

1

*I stored you against my eyelids*
*my treasure, more precious than water.*

> *Then they stole my home, my land,*
> *the possibility of my hands, my last dress.*

*I saw them, and when my eyes closed*
*I could not remember you.*

*Hunger has eaten my dreams.*
*You are a scarecrow in a field*
> *the birds have plundered – useless love.*
> *Send money; I cannot eat your pink words.*

*The moon will not believe me.*
*She says my heart is beating in your vanished hands.*

2

This woman walking along the road
keeps seeing her heart fall behind her
bleeding into the buried caul.

This woman walking along the road keeps walking.

Her heart keeps falling away from her.

She roasts the falling heart on tinder fires
to sell to hungry travellers.

She dreams of arms wrapped around arms.

She dreams she is a feather on a flying bird.

She dreams of an enormous mother beckoning her.

She carries her father on her journey's back.

Her stomach is filled with his bones.

She bursts with pain and continues walking.

Her heart drops away, drops away.

She calls 'I love you' in the wind.

The words hang like dead birds around her ears.

She is a stick no one will hold.

    Far away, her name has faded on a man's dry skin.

She lies down on the gravel.

A thorn tree grows through her,
pushing her upright.

3

The woman with the thorn tree growing through her chest
                                        arrives in the city.
She sees a picture of a house with grass and water,
and a doorway in which people embrace.
She decides to become such a house.
She sits on the sandy floor of the city.

She plucks an orange from the gutter and sells it to a hungry man.

    A man grabs the orange and eats it fast,
    thinking the taste of the woman seller.
    It wasn't enough.

She has six cents in her hand, she shows it to the moon.

4

*The moon curses me, turning away*
*and I juggle with oranges in the dirt.*
*I juggle with coins I plaster my skin with hands.*
*The moon curses me, returning.*

*Everyone is hungry, every mouth eats me.*
*I am only so many crumbs of air, a sky*
*covered with ants, they carry me piece by piece away.*
*The moon stays, stroking the black bone beneath.*

*What if I had waited for him on the road?*
*Moon, you know nothing.*
*My hands held no offering for him.*
*I am cursed with myself.*

5

Trader in hungers,
she grew strong.

And everything that could be eaten, was eaten.

She was bricks, words, skin, bread.

She was fire, milk, the road, the shade.

Her roof stretched wide across the city.

In her doorway people embraced.

The moon grew thinner and thinner
watching over the wastelands of her abundance.

6

*Ghost against trees, lucent hunger
or thirst? Is it silver water
that would bring you back to me?*

*I am dry sticks, my love,
and I hunger so for the greenness
of hands on me, I am the carcass of dreams,
you may drift through my spaces.*

*Where do you sleep,
who do you love,
are you somewhere else a man?
Transparent love, your body*

*holds my earth and sky,
you are the window open on my drought.*

*You are a dead ghost.
I am rich and you will eat none of my coins.
You are a memory ghost.
Nothing is promised me.
From hunger to wealth I have come
through the desert of my heart.*

## Needle work

From my needle small birds fly:
pink lattice feathers, leafgreen eyes,
yellow crests, plum spikes for tails.

Beside me on the metal pole
tubing threads down from a plastic bag
thick and soft as a pound of liver:

your blood, midnight red stitches
of the deep needle filling you;
mine chainstitching bright birds.

## I WHO LIVE HERE, IT IS I

> *'This earth was the first to speak.*
> *I have been pronounced once and for all.'*
> — Breyten Breytenbach, *Return to Paradise*

*1*

In my sleep I return here.

\*

Being here, giving birth to my city I am
day by day being home, day by day
it has no name, seeds came from all parts of the known world
to plant me here, being myself these rooms, streets, rain, tides,
the air tasting of me, cool mist my hair, my skin hot stone,
the pulsing of hands my hands growing sand and wood
as the sky enters my eyes and the sea wells from my feet
and I turning inside out disappear into all manner of joyous
                                                bird cries
and the weeping of engines and wind,
gulls and avid rats feed where I feed,
consuming this limitless home swelling inside me
as I inside it open wide enough to die.

\*

Coming home I see it coming towards me,
rubbing against me like a welcoming cat.

In my sleep I feel it leaning against me, sleeping.

\*

Dried apricots, soft and sour
dawn wind stings the palm tree.

Neon rivers spilling across
the smell of buses pushing homeward.

*

In my sleep I return here.

2

It is only one look, one acrid glance shearing across
                                      the sweet blue hour
and the air pulls back, embarrassed at its intimacy,
leaving me naked as a captured slave, a trespasser, a thief.

All people ask: what are you doing here? what are you?
Eyes and eyes and eyes, scraping my shadow off all surfaces.

Any person here rebukes me.
Any person here in the streets of my home rebukes me.
I, walking like a strange person in the streets of my home
stare at my footsteps spread out on the road and deny them.
Any person is more at home here than I am.

The walls and the wind withdraw obediently from my skin.
I breathe in the bitter juice of any person looking at me,
peeling me off the air, expelling me.

All people live in my home and say it is not me, it is not,
all people invite me in and say look, it is not yours, welcome.

Any person has permission because of history.
Because of justice. Because of songs of genesis.
Any person being decidedly here in my self
banishes me. Any person refuses permission.
Any person who says nothing, or everything,
does not say my name. Any person is here in my place,
it is not my place.

How is it that my born home
is loyal to anyone who passes
in the street, following him like a hot beast
eager for better origins?

3

They say if my name were found here
buried in rock older and older
than any home a person can recall,
my home would return to me.

But no name is my home.
I am spread wider over the sand
than the width of a name.
Being born here the cells of my skin
are all the time of history.

What voice could pronounce the whole tide of my days?
What eyes could pour sky into my sky?

If this could be, if anyone here
were here with me inside the water and the wind
my home would flow through me and through anyone
and return to me, return to me in my sleep.

## Dispossessed words

*(Found poem)*

*For Jessie Tamboer, who set herself alight and burned to death because she could no longer provide food for her children*

Trucks carried 40 000 blacks to the southern edge of the
                                                        desert.
I cannot say anything about my future now.
    We had a very beautiful view
    and this was the first time I saw my father cry.

They said 'Old man, are you moving?'
I took a crowbar, pulled the house down.
I cannot say anything about my future now.

      *

    A man must have a dumping ground.
    Every rabbit has got a warren.
    A native must have a warren too.

      *

Sometimes I cry, I
the absolute poor
I am sick to death of watching my ruin.

      *

We had a very beautiful view of the sea –
    this was refused.

    *

Uncovering rubbish bins, I ask, could it not be
that something has been thrown in here –
just a little something that I can chew?

This was refused.

    *

At times she would just suddenly start sobbing
without any apparent reason.

The absence of love.
There is no way you can describe that hunger.
Shining clean pots and jars:
there was no food whatsoever in the house.

    *

She was immediately engulfed by flames
    but did not utter a sound
as she walked around the yard burning.

The ashes of one household are collected by another
for the bits of coal.
If you want to survive you must make a plan.

I cannot say anything about my future now.

## Leader

In these plague nights he lays his body open
to the infinite small creatures needing his blood.

The air is dense with mists of sentiment
circling the mounds of opalescent eggs
laid upon altars, over graves, along the great road,
lifting their silvery mucus like wedding veils.

Inside each one, foetal and perfectly formed,
power grows with the softness of insect wings,
incubating in the sweet clouds that thicken
over his open body.

## Reclaiming our land

Every map is out of date.
The roads go to unbuilt houses.
How do the tortoises know
there's bush on the far side of the tar?

At night stars fall like gooseberries,
one into my lap, one into your lap,
husked in cosmic permissions.
Everyone gets a star.
Soon there'll be none left.
You have to eat it; they aren't for planting.

Put up a mirror where you are
and make yourself at home in your familiar eyes.
Outside the wind blew it all away.

## Incarnate Eternity

arrive screaming
in this blood-birth
steel and the roses in my eyes
nor any grief will still me
not for your most holy suffering will I lay down
my wings in this necessary massacre
with all my life seizing the jasmine growing
from the hole where they raped me
how it grows and grows

\*

        (that pastel hope
        is an old sweet wrapper:
        burn it, your teeth are stained
        with mourning)

\*

blood is good for you
it is above all something red and liquid
like a strawberry in a shaft of sunlight

it wells up through bones and tissue
clotted with boundaries of hair and white fluids
this is the place the sun hides at night
bring it out, melt my hands with it

the ritual is to pour a cup
of someone's blood onto the land,
this is your way of claiming your home,
your political truth, your existence

kiss me, my lips are full of it,
I live here

*

red river, you smell of freedom
as the new grass smells of my father's bones

*

my arm uncurls
and I am holding for you
grown out of all the spores of my generations
the green territory of the fern they planted in my kloof –
look how the red drops from it!

*

it is
the bridge of blood        two little souls crossing
                                                       under a parasol
the barrier of blood      the tidal wave is a wall of fish
the big red full stop       the maize grows so tall
                                                       this yellow year
the juice of vote papers    beetles scavenge like jewels

quickred
seasalted
here even the shadows bleed
especially the shadows bleed
dark sponges of history
birds suck from them
in the drought growing fat, red

\*

To be here is my breast in my hand
aimed at you, my cannibal happiness,
your wail dismembering the road
but when the red train passes into my tunnel
something opens : time : silence
the linear serenity of air against this cool mountain
space beyond blood, my ocean spreads.

Abandon me to this blue present.

Where I sit permanence shimmers
and my heart is a cave the birds leave and enter.
Now you may slice off my head,
my neck spills pearls and the breath of whales,
my spine rolls against a silver hand,
my fingers are grains of sand.
This beak pecking my lips
this beak pecking my lips
draws blood whose blood is in me
how did the ocean get this red?

\*

We are showing ourselves to ourselves
the people of our future
agonies of half-bodies
watching each other across a blade.
Are you lost? come home now.

The human hand can exert force of eight litres per bullet
and so light on its toes.

Oh mother, mother, why are you crying?
She looks just like you.
Here, let me take this blood off your lap.

>―<*

>―<Sit absolutely still
>―<as they sever your selves
>―<sit absolutely still
>―<bleed precisely downward
>―<concentrate your spirit
>―<into this pillar of memory
>―<no one passing through
>―<will survive.

| | |
|---|---|
| I have been walking | I have been sitting on one side |
| I have been watching | I have been waiting on one side |
| I have been undoing | I have been in the water |
| I have been not waiting | I have been walking |
| I have been unfolding | I have been filling my shadow |

>―<here it comes
>―<I had no name for calling it
>―<here it comes
>―<red juice of the future
>―<pouring me out

what can you do?
>―<can you do this, too?
>―<faster, faster

>―<*

*Homework*:

        *categories:*

           blood

| | | | | |
|---|---|---|---|---|
| relation | kin | bloodshed | sap | life force |
| family | culture | slaughter | liquid | heart's blood |
| breed | tribe | slaying | gore | own flesh |
| seed | clan | extermination | own flesh | |
| own flesh | own flesh | own flesh | | |

## Tiresias in the city of heroes

*1  In the city of heroes*

Not only the unexploded bombs in their hearts
but these sweet pools of honey in each pair of hands
cupped to sip, being
a past that lit the night all the way to this
ending: dry air in a still, old city.

Memories are the daylight, in a place with no present.
The map with the closed rooms along the way unfolded
and you arrived with all the closed rooms in your years
throbbing, you arrived beyond the boundary of your map
saying, here I am, and from the closed rooms
such voices answered you: here I am.

If they had known the script
these heroes in the city of heroes
would have become statues and stopped waiting.

As it is they sat so still all day
but not – composed,
something in the angles of the amputated limbs
always implying movement of the ghost of movement,
even though absent, not finished yet


\*

waiting.

\*

Over the square the pale dust of the dry season sifts;
from jacarandas and flamboyants desiccated petals
in the victory colours fall.
Air murmurs.

The jungle licks the walls on the home side;
reticent waves attend at the outer edge.

The ground transmits biographies
of movement and hesitation,
vibrations of uneven footsteps circling
this city, this transit camp, this photograph of the time
before the end of struggle,
souvenir of the old days,
still breathing.

The jungle rustles with satisfied laughter.
It opens no path, yields no messenger,
darker and darker green, ancient.

\*

After the war there are always heroes
to be forgotten until they are dead.
There can be no heroes in times of peace.
Inside every song the words are buried:
Stay away, heroes of our struggles.
Let us paint pictures of you, let us tell stories.
Stay away where we can imagine you.
If you return now you will crumble like ancient kings
untombed in our corrosive air.

\*

These are not refugees, good god –
it isn't help they need, coins and crutches.
These men and women left in a column of fire
and will return garlanded with their deeds.
These men and women went in order to return,
not fleeing they were singing the jungles open,
setting up mirrors all the way to look back,
to send light and their faces back to the homeland
waiting for their deeds to arrive.
Not seeing the jungle grow up in their mirrors
new and permanent.

*

These heroes are heroes,
triumphant on the long, long way home,
their silent days in this city
are a journey and it will end.

> And they will become kings and queens
> in their own land,
> and multitudes will welcome them
> with candles and flowers and firstborn children
> to bless with their golden pain.

2   *Tiresias remembers*

A man came, unfortunate bridge. Tiresias:
with his dangerous memory come to the city of heroes.
Foolish man, looking for a woman
to watch her say again, go away.
Melting memories into dreams with a blind longing,
the hot longing that opens darkness,

melting the dreams of heroes into memories,
aching, aching.

       \*

A man arriving is an emissary or an enemy.
Tiresias holds his poor broken heart under the shedding
                                     jacaranda
as the heroes undo him with questions.

'Tell us the story of the war we won.'
Like children looking for a history to wear.

What do I remember? Standing in the sun for hours listening to speeches while my feet burned on the ground. Walking along streets where women stood at every door crying. Hacked bodies. A little man who followed me for three kilometres and when I finally tried to grab him he begged me to teach him to sing, but I thought he was lying and killed him. A baby with its stomach carved out and a policeman standing next to it, vomiting. Being given a computer and told to write. The smell of beer on dead men's lips. Sitting in a shebeen drinking brandy after brandy and getting so happy I felt like flying. A woman laughing as another woman's house burned down. Yellow cars and vans: that thick flat yellow like sweet icing on a cake. The noise of helicopters. My mother saying don't go, or don't come back. My child screaming when I tried to pick him up. Meat roasting at my child's funeral. A book with my photo in it. Crowds becoming silent. A man who shot his wife in a meeting. The noise of helicopters. My burning feet. Bodies in the street covered in blankets. My home is a place I'm frightened of. It's a big sore inside me that burns when I touch it.

'Are you not bigger than your own backyard?
In that war each of us became the nation:
the whole nation entered into each of us.
Tell us that story.'

That story. That story:
In Sharpeville your arms died.
In Uitenhage your tongues died.
In Boipatong your eyes died.
In Katlehong and Bekkersdal and Empangeni
you died and you died and you died.
That's what I remember.

In Pretoria your fingernails became joint chief of staff.
In Pretoria your teeth ran the central bank.
In Pretoria your hair was the president.
That's what I remember.

In Joburg your heart was tortured and died.
In Cape Town your skin joined the enemy police.
In the veld and the mountains your memory buried
                                      its children.
That's what I remember.

That's what I remember.
All this dead and defeated, is your story.
Only the hair and the shadow still growing,
responding to sunlight, and I ask myself
which body were they grafted onto,
in that moment of darkness
before total victory was declared?
My home is a place I'm frightened of.

The heroes leave him in the marketplace
like an old newspaper, blurred with the truth,
sifting the dry breeze for her scent.

*

In a cool room she lies on the mourning mat.
Themba, he says, Themba, Themba.
You are still here.

You are still here, she says with the voice of dead bullets.
He is gone and you are still here.
Why couldn't they kill you?

*

There's nothing to remember.
What remains is here.
Its origins will repeat themselves.
How this man got his power
and that man starves
will not glue joy to your heart.
Sing or dream
or keep silent inside your bandages.
Don't dig, it only cuts the roots
and whatever is growing now will wither
like what came before.
Silence is big enough to hold the present
wide open for you to breathe in.

*

## 3  To save what must be saved

Heroes are those who will kill to save what must be saved.

Mnyaniso comes to the doorstep where Tiresias sits
carrying the knife, the long curved blade,
a hook for a man's heart.
Once before he has excised a heart from his body
unmarked and fresh, a bulb stored
in the dark room of his return.

'Ah, Mnyaniso, do you remember
how as a child you could carve open the stem of a lily
without snapping it? How the lily continued to grow,
receiving its sap in two rivers now instead of one?'

'We could do such things, such things, Tiresias,
such expansions of the spirit in us.
Now my hand is a vulture on my dead days.'

'But remember, Mnyaniso, remember your hand, remember.'

All night Mnyaniso cut the bougainvillea petals,
and in the morning Tiresias was a tree
with a million blood-red birds singing in its branches.

from *The Canary's Songbook*

(2005)

## Broken bits of the past

Broken bits of the past
find their way into my pockets

bright as the eyes of stray dogs,
pleading and fierce.

In sympathy the present hammers itself to pieces
and climbs in there.

Cement – we need cement now,
wood glue, paper glue, fixatives, bonding agents,

they should issue all schoolchildren with enough,
send them back to the land

to cement it in place, cement down their parents,
make plaster casts of bones to bury there as ancestors,

order indigenous trees from catalogues
and plant them everywhere to stabilise the sand,

bury the smashed masks and pots
deep in the ground to keep it drained,

feed the dogs and send them on their way,
settle things, settle them down once and for all.

# Knocking Series

*1   So you begin*

So you begin by arriving
at a front door.

You hear a sound like water falling,
but the walls of the house are dry.

Knock, or listen carefully
standing to one side, in shadow.

Will you be recognised?
Is your name known here?

You must knock, the only way out
is through this door.

The forest is all around you
and if your house is here

then surely it is the forest where you live?
Surely your shadow will know its way

among the old low swaying branches,
among the fresh leaves and broken twigs

pointing backwards and forwards?

## 2 *Walls of wisteria*

Walls of wisteria waylay me everywhere.
I'm trying to find my way to the wild place
where drums summon the dead to speak
but the wisteria captures me in sweetness
and I can't pass through.

I tear at the blossoms, looking for thorn trees locked
                                          in dry earth.
Beyond the soft clusters are hedges of rosebuds,
beyond them the olive and almond trees amble,
beyond them the boundary of cypresses stands guard
implacably peaceful.

I light fires in the meadow with the songs of tall
                                          desert women,
but the wisteria lays its lilac light over my skin,
the cypresses send a mist of songbirds through my hair,
the roses bring my mother and father to me in dreams
so that I'll stay here.

## 3 *Taller than my shadow*

When I go home to honour my ancestors
they gather round me like hitchhikers
clamouring to join me on my travels.

I say to them what is the best way?
and they always answer:
you will show us.

Year by year I grow taller
and the bag on my back grows heavier
with wriggling ghosts.

At night the ancestors pay their way
by sending me dreams.
I wake having been in so many former living rooms

I have no idea how to redecorate my house
or what to do with the garden,
and several letters of apology seem necessary.

## Treasure Trail

How did you know?
I find them now

as I need them:
the Neruda volume,

the Zen anthology,
the Horowitz recordings.

You laid a trail quietly
and left, left your warm gown,

left the incense wrapped in thin paper,
the matches in your pocket, still dry.

I remember the saxophone you sold
before I was born.

When I hear it now
I know I'm walking in the right direction.

I look up and see you on the horizon,
walking along it, looking for something.

## Stones for my Pockets

Burying our mothers one by one
we float away,

the good girls and the bad girls.
No one will ever ask again,

when are you coming home?
All the suitcases empty themselves and leave us.

After the first freefall hours of grief
we'll become sirens or sibyls, ageless, untouchable.

One friend captures her mother's hands again and again
on cloth, glass, paper.
One pins down with words a certain neatness of the eyes,
a certain folded pain.
One spins her babies into swirls of paint petals
in their grandmother's autumn.

I collect your stories,
stones for my pockets
to hold me down
when the root goes.

## Men wear the secret masks

Men wear the secret masks
and blow the flutes.
These are the voices of ancestral birds
singing of their warrior deeds.

The women must never see
the men blowing their flutes.
If a woman sees the bird
become a man, he kills her.

This happens in every house.
There is always an ancestral bird
in the shape of a man
singing in the shape of a flute.

There is always a woman
seeing something that could kill her.

# In Jakob's House

*1*

On one morning, Jakob, holding my hand
though I was holding yours, you took me
from my first apple and honey breakfast
among Rodchenko's functional dreams,
through the heroin-haunted station
into your most recent city.

We wandered between galleries of life-size traps
for animals and people built of recycled materials,
down a long dinner table of sculpted silent men,
through open-legged streets of Japanese whore-children
pinned to the walls and out into the medieval square
where roasted almonds, gingerbread and spiced wine
played their flutes around your voice
leading me further than I had come.

Pierced by the winter sun's bleak eyes we sat
bare-headed drinking coffee after coffee,
watching the exiled Roma women
perform their desperation for us.

Inside your unfolding story of the century's failure
you ushered me past the monumental mechanical worker
striking the air over the heads of Frankfurt's electronic
                                                  princes,
through scaffold towers and across pavements drilled open
to receive new steel roots, into the darkness
of the tiny shop where chocolates are made
according to a treasured recipe, and chose
ten small perfections for your anxious beloved.

Jakob, how many worlds have you survived?
I know you only in swallow swoops inside a few journeys,
drinking briefly from the small bowls you leave
in places I might pause to sip.

You've read everything and you're out walking to work
in your eighty-sixth year, in this century full of dying struggles
you step surefooted into the next skyscraper shadow
convinced that human beings are still growing towards
                                                  the sun.

Were you always this wholehearted?
Did you stand on a silent threshold one year
looking at your bombed past and grow
thinner than unfed dogs in the frozen street?

You are the century that rescued Europe from itself,
the man who still carries Kristallnacht's splinters in his pocket,
who's read the bankers' ransom notes to governments
and the eyes of women with drugged babies
invading suburban trains, Kandinsky's colours
and Bill Viola's roaring brain music,
and who draws his comrades of all countries
into the late November wind
to review their mistakes and plan their next campaign.

Leaving again for my southern home
I think about the first journey of a family
that did not have the strength to carry you
inside its memories, inside its hopes.
May I choose you now, Jakob, as my father's father,
the one he never knew? Is it too late?

2

In Jakob's house I feel welcome.
And it is Sigi's house and it is she who welcomes me
inside her diamond-cutter's gaze,
letting Jakob's story fill the air like incense,
her own smoke curling privately along the walls.
She's chosen this, it suits her
to be left out of the light
that washes what she's seen away from itself.

Sometimes she brings a quiet set of inverted commas
out of her smile to place around him.
Often she shakes her head as he talks.
Her life is full of the history
he hopes will lead to better things.

Through my guest room walls
their voices come during the night,
tumbling embrace of Schumann's cadences,
braced spine of Brecht's chords.

3

Dear Jakob, where I come from there are men like you
but their memories are shorter. They read no poetry
because the distances are too great between hunger and a plan.
Wide-eyed with commitment, stopping nowhere long enough.

Where I live time is so new that those in power
wear gold-plated watches bigger than their hearts.
Your continent's horrors were my childhood fables.

Mine come roaring at me in three dimensions of sunlit misery
louder than my language. Here love is never
the answer to anyone's weeping

and I hunger so for that landscape of intimate struggles,
willingness to save one person at a time.
Easily seduced by darkness stories
offered like bitter chocolate in a bright room,
my longings twine around the wrought-iron ruins of lives
fire-bombed into a lacework of suffering,
wrapped in old furs and the loyalty of candlelit shelters,
full of a cabaret melancholy I swallow like red wine.
A history filled with matinee idols rushing to rescue me
from the utter loneliness of my dreams.

Who are you loyal to, Jakob,
who would you say no to, for whose sake?
You have a kindness inside your anger
that makes your violent century bearable
but you are a man like a man I know
and I must ask you this, forgive me Jakob,
who have you destroyed by not looking back?

It is your work to keep walking
sweet-voiced and urgent ahead of your children.
Your house is full of love and its walls are made only
                                                   of thoughts,
and you will keep leaving to go to work and returning
to build new walls against the winds that follow you

and under the bare sky of the future
I will shelter in my heart
the small nest of history you built for me there.

## Ox blood poisons the ground with longing

Ox blood poisons the ground with longing
for better times long gone.

Through the suburban streets the lowing of beasts
                                          before death
shadows the grass verges and turns the jacarandas red.

Even those who never knew where to pour their libations
understand that there were things they should have asked

of the spirits in another language now lost to everyone
except the oxen walking between cars

to die here,
knowing it is no use.

The words in their blood run away into the tar
as soon as their faithful necks are slashed open.

## Visiting home

In a lull,
on a low-news long weekend,
the president goes home to propitiate
(thank, ask, apologise, libate)
his ancestors.

His mother sighs and orders cattle
for the slaughter ceremony,
the villagers and media crews,
and Jik for the blood.

What else to do?
It is, after all, the story of the past.
Times do come when this story is
urgently needed.

So if the president can fit in now
a digitisation of the old home movie,
we should take advantage of the moment.
He's doing it for all of us.

The air will be disturbed
and afterwards will settle,
and whatever was in the air
hoping or watching –

the curious wind,
and the president's mother's memories
as she washes the sheets and hangs them in the sun,
the ones the president slept on as a child.

## The Personal Assistant

Smaller than a paper clip
magnetised
with tips that extend
silently
or in the dark,

inside his master's armour
he runs up and down
working the levers.

He's the one to be careful of,
the one without the speeches,
the one who keeps the borders open
between yes and no.

He knows spells that only work
in silence, or in the dark,
for bringing armies to their knees.
Sunlight obeys him, and building plans.

With a signature, a date, a key turned or lost
he conquers countries and your fate before breakfast
and returns them apparently unharmed
to his master for the meeting,
the press conference, the handshake.

## Redistributing It

Water sloshes over into the new hollows
finding its level again
and the weight of it lies a little differently
over the earth.
Stolen air is swallowed now in different corridors,
the map of suffocation redraws itself.

The dogs track theft's footprints steadfastly
through offices and parliaments.
These cupboards splintered by laws,
these gardens carried away as evidence.
Bring the food trucks and the milk trucks
to this side now.

Mass death has moved in here,
the groaning old woman in the child's house,
and the child at the door looking out
with her wide clean eyes like empty bowls,
and the dogs moving past,
noses to the perfumed road.

## Oral Tradition

He's heard the stories
of a century of slow pain,
slow struggle, slow change
slipping back every day.

The wind blowing down everything built,
the bruised bodies, the jerseys with holes in them.

This boy does skyscraper deals at the speed of sound
and they hold, they seem to hold.
In six months he's accumulated
more than his parents' bosses earned in a lifetime.

Where are the old slow forces
that moved barefoot across stones and years?

This boy's mind seems light and strong
in the way that a plane's wings are strong,
flexible, familiar with moving air,
with the wind's flight paths.

He has such weak legs,
he will never be able to walk away from the crash site.

## Flakes of the light falling

*(Plague poem)*

approximately and here also
one in four vanishing
even as we speak –

lightly and without technique they are dying
slowly and beyond the duration of love

good citizens of a good country, dying modestly
embrace of the infected is a national project
rejection the prerogative of the intimate circle

metaphors of love crack open,
out of their varnished shells
people emerge, dying

howling is not possible where children sleep
and their mothers, dying blossoms of blue light
inside the cloudbursts of men's love

very close to the ground children and their mothers
and then also their fathers die here
in the way of poor people, struggling
for small dignities and the simplest food
astonished softly over and over
I touch my lips to each death

approximately and here also
one in four vanishing –

how many little pallbearers for one coffin?
to wrap your father in a sheet takes days and days
tangling yourself in the web of bones
who will bury him if you don't?
you saw helplessly at the tree

all night my little clock makes a vastly solemn noise
like a child treading the long dark passage
in her grandfather's shoes

among blades of grass, against crumbled walls
let cows offer their udders to the babies
lying upturned, helpless as beetles

metaphors of love crack open

suddenly one day you will hear
how silently the black sky blazes
how wildly the empty street is searching
for a footstep

we are ending, we are ending
flakes of the light falling away

# Book

*page 1*

Here you are. Will you go further?

*page 2*

A small rabbit sits in the middle of a road.

What do you think of when you read this?

Perhaps the flat stretch between Laingsburg and Beaufort
West,
the roadworks, the ostriches that come over the hill
to stare at the waiting cars.

Perhaps night, the rabbit's eyes shining.

Perhaps what you did in a car once on that road, also at night,
with a wonderful man, driving at very high speed.

Think of the little rabbit on the white line.
Cars are thundering by.

*page 3*

It's early morning, whisperstill.
Walking in the veld
a man was touched on one side
by the palest light.

Look back.
Can you still see the road?

*page 4*

Pushed into a clump of thorn bushes
a hut clutches at the spines of shade.
No clues about the owner, though this is private land.
There's one like it on every page
without windows, a doorway with no door.

If you wait here someone might come.
The hut looks abandoned
but there's a canvas bag against one wall.
You could wait, or move on.
That might be breath you hear, or the sound of footsteps.

*page 5*

Standing near a barbed wire fence
why do you have the feeling
something bad happened here
once or many times?

You know more about this place than you can explain.

*page 6*

What are you thinking of?
When you look at this hill
knowing which country you're in,
what images spread themselves on the ground
among the splintered pink stones scattered everywhere,
softening the light?

*page 7*

This is a very barren place.
Dreaming doesn't make it better.

You could watch a *film noir* on television.
When it was over your room would feel brighter, gentler –
a nest of yellow cushions.

Out here the sounds and textures challenge your skin
to grow scales, or feathers. Learn to caw, to hiss, to buzz
between the mimosa petals spattered with your blood.

But you can walk here. Your boots won't go through the page.

*page 8*

Is the rabbit still there?
Is it alive?
You can't sit in the hut forever.

To find out would mean going back.

*page 9*

So, you landed in a rabbit's story
on a national road
in a wide country.

Not even water was provided.

Or stories about lives
a little like yours.
Someone whose heart was bruised

like yours by someone
like someone you love.
Not a rabbit, unless
it has a soul like yours,
unless it is a symbol.
Are you perhaps a symbol for the rabbit?

*page 10*

A road and a stretch of veld
unspooled
across a blank page.

Cars and plants in a landscape.

If the rabbit is still there
it is by now flecked flesh and blood
staining the paper.

Were you there?
Did you come back?

## Walking songs for Africans abroad

*A travelling game*

There's a game we play when we travel abroad.
Looking up from a drink in a bar, a museum queue,
                              a souvenir counter
we ask, where are the Africans?

We ask, where are the Africans?
And we answer each other in different ways
depending on the mood we're in.
It's a way to pass through the hours of estrangement,
a way to walk through the galleries of strange looks
                              from strangers.

The game ends when one of us says,
that's a non-question.

Or when we realise there are non-African friends among us
looking hurt, or starting to apologise for something.
We change the subject then. It's seldom worth the effort
of trying to explain this isn't about them.

One of us alone may ask the question silently
stepping out into the morning of a foreign city,
like a ghost setting out to haunt an unfamiliar house.
It's a way of comforting ourselves, recalling that there must be
other ghosts like us, and that we all haunt houses
where we've never lived.

*At Lago di Garda they have other problems*

Lago di Garda is a beautiful place,
laced with settings for Goethe's dreams of the south.
Walking along the narrow road between Sompriezzo and Pieve
you understand at last the things in your childhood
$$\text{anthologies:}$$
cowbells, hazelnut trees, Jews hidden in caves and barns,
$$\text{bramble berries.}$$

Around the lake itself cypresses preen,
lemon groves pretend an ancient elegance
and the *gelati* are pistachio, vanilla, cherry and lime
just as they should be.
I looked around unrestfully, not knowing why.
The light was chiffon everywhere, a kind of silence
filtering the chatter of the promenade away from
$$\text{anything true.}$$

I thought I saw a dark shape walking up a side street
and my skin changed as if someone familiar had touched me.
But it was gone, or never there –
only the cool palazzo walls stared past me.
I knew I must be the only person in this whole town
who could even imagine what my real world is like,
so much light and earth, so much sleeping and growing.

But later I watched the tired owner of the *gelateria* locking
$$\text{his doors}$$
and realised he'd probably been trying to speak German
$$\text{all day to Bavarian tourists.}$$
Nobody really cares what anyone else's world is like, unless
$$\text{they're writing a PhD.}$$
It's not a crime against humanity.

*Thesaurus entries for 'Africans abroad'*

in transit
transitory
transitional
transient

*The sociological fraud*

If you ask the wrong question, you get the wrong answer.
An African taught me that.

I ask them anyway, when I get lonely.
The answers astonish each time, like onions.

For example:
Why is the first human you see at any airport
a black man handling luggage?

Why do American novelists still divide their characters
into 'characters' and 'black characters'?

Why are there no African skinheads or *au pairs*?

*At conferences we learn so much*

To stand inside your theories, unuttered,
produces a dizziness. Caught between the lushness
                              of my world
and its absence here. Do you think your ruling class's
                              surplus capital
came from a hole in the ground in Greenland?

Talking and talking you talk, my dedicated friends,

and all that you know teeters on a point of blindness
your toes fail to sense, clutching the soles of your feet,
thinking they are the whole earth's curve supporting you.

Local rabbits in smart jeans, you're thermally well-protected
                                  and anxious for change,
just checking the time on your perfect watches.
Do you ever look at your backs in the mirror?
From my country we see them all the time,
the raw edges, the sand trickling out of the seams, the
                                  drought-stricken heels.
Millions of tiny seamstresses still working on you.

You welcome us, we are your cautionary tales,
your myths, your keynote speakers,
the parts of you that walked across the mined desert
                                  to get here.
You wish you could have a miracle like ours,
a sort of atom bomb of festivity to clear the past out of
                                  the way.

The puzzled looks on our faces you take for a problem
                                  of language,
and devote yourselves to whispering translations of the
                                  speeches in our ears.
You're right, in a sense; we don't have a language for saying
where do your questions come from?

Hanging around in corners like one of Jane Austen's
                                  minor girls,
I'm trying to tuck my continent in behind me
so no one trips on it. But it's so damned big.
I should never have tried to bring it with me.

'Wear ethnic dress,' they ask all delegates.
As if history were a diorama in a department store window
and not the bright patterns of blood on all our
                                                bedroom floors.
Their ethnic dress is black leather with a touch of something
striped. Nepalese, Guatemalan. Very cool.

*Born travellers*

We're born travellers. We compose walking songs, songs of
building the boss's roads, songs of the long train journey to
the mines, songs of our lovers abandoning us for city women,
songs of living in hostels without our children, of standing at
passport offices, of being in exile, of tracking a cow or a lion
or a USAID management studies programme. We invented a
piano the size of our hearts to play as we walk.

We've been travelling forever. There's a map that shows
how Africans spread across the world to populate it; the
cartographers called it 'Africans: the first colonisers'.
Some of us have objected to being called that. We're more
comfortable with the modest role of loving our birthplace
and wanting it back. But we keep on travelling, in the holds
of ships and down mine shafts, with crates of goods to sell
and dossiers of crimes to recount. We have so much left to
give, so many blood diamonds and bleached bones, so many
muted languages and ecstatic dances. Over and over again we
repopulate the world with our evolving pain and curiosity,
replenishing each present moment with the DNA of history.

*'At the round earth's imagined corners'*

After another one of those trips
someone sees his colleague at the airport queuing
                              for the pay phone
and says, 'E T phone home ...'
and she says, 'This *is* home, aren't we the world's brothers
                                          and sisters?'
and he says, 'Tell that to the passport officers'
and they laugh, and inside they each feel a little sick,
and on the plane each one wakes at some point during
                                      the flight
to jot down a few words in a diary, notes for a song or a poem.

## Globalisation

*1*

From a distance
everyone looks human.

Even the gun-toting weebly-wobbly doll
in his tight shoes, with his handlers.

Even the dark-eyed dragon watching
all kinds of prophetic chickens come home to roost
                                        in his beard.

Even the bundle of melted flesh
lying at an angle to its wailing father.

From a distance you think –
there's someone I know, I'll wave, I'll invite him in for coffee.

*2*

Loudly you fall over me like bricks
with your song of growth
through loans through contracts through programmes
poured down the boreholes of conditionalities
your system digs through this continent.
In the earthquake of your voice I crack and collapse
and all that protects me now is this whispered No,
this small air pocket I live in.

## Aching

If I could just
catch the man falling
there, so high, so tiny

if I could just
push my hand through the screen
into the burning city

I'd be bleeding, he'd be screaming,
the terror would be real
inside, here

there's smoke and ash pushing against the glass
trying to reach me –

Or if I come outside,
lie down in the wet grass until my skin shivers,
smell the green night rubbing my cheeks

if in the sky over Refrontolo
a satellite can find me, take my picture,
show it to the people in New York

who'll lean towards their screens fascinated, aching
through this distance –

*

In Frankfurt I stand one arm's length
from a woman on display
and in my chest a burning grows

that I mistake for sadness and then recognise as shame.

No one should come this close
even to the bronze and oil paint simulacrum of a moment
of such detailed inwardness. Every fold and freckle of her
                                                    sagging face
stands still for me to catalogue. This pain cracking my heart
                                                    open

is the artist's trick. He's pushed me through the screen.
The woman's eyes refuse mine, her lips stay closed.
The words that name me come out of my own mouth:
Housebreaker. Violator. Thief.

\*

Don't stare, it's rude.
And empathy is rape.
And kindness is, like hunger, loss of self.

What is the right distance for touching?

They say if you want a dog to come to you
stand still, don't run towards it, calling.

And when it comes?

## Soft

Soft on a summer bed in the Languedoc
a man in an Afghan prison sits with me
watching his brother walking through snowdrifts
to a village much like this one
(*boucherie*, *tabac*, *boulangerie*, broken shutters)
where a month's supply of bullets lies secured
in a box beneath his mother's wedding carpet.

Turning the pages of Bruce Chatwin's life
I feel the ashy bodies shift and stutter downward
through steel sticks broken on New York's southern streets.
Peruvian feathers hang in coloured blocks
across the whiteness of a wall in England,
the man in the snow takes another step forward,
under a sky-blue *burqa* a woman writes to the man in prison
without pen or paper.

Together we turn the pages, always together now.
Lavender. Ash. Snow on a black beard.

*Marseillette – Kabul – New York, September 2001*

## A CERTAIN HISTORY

Dust is shy,
like fallen hair.

Together they go
to the shelter of corners,

gathering in small furry stillnesses
like servants of the deceased at a funeral,

or drift up a lampstand,
across the top of an armchair,

waiting to be removed.
In the empty late afternoon sunlight

they float unobserved, gold shimmering mosaics inlaid in air
as if by artists of rare skill, celebrating a certain history.

## The canary's songbook

The incredibly cheerful canary
hasn't stopped singing all morning
out of her cage at last, down here
among the dark wetly alluring rocks
in the long mysteriously endless tunnel.

She's free and she sings
every song she remembers
and others she's never heard before
and she takes no notice of the people passing
who say 'oh no, not another canary metaphor',
she's having such a good time,
she's having the time of her life.

Her songbook is as old as the hills
and as familiar as birds chattering
and footsteps marching past.
She's learning it page by page,
amazed that her voice knows the way.

She could have been a rosebush facing a row of vines,
dying ahead of them in a cloud of eager fungus
to save their precious skins

but she'd rather be down here among the rocks
that flash their gold smiles in the pool of darkness
she stares into, thinking she sees a beautiful canary there.

You have to imagine her in the tunnel singing
and the wet rocks shining
and the men retreating to safety.

from *Slowly, As If*

(2012)

## Cyrus Vance sat on my couch

Cyrus Vance sat on my couch,
the curved pale blue one with the coffee stain
that Saul and David left behind in the Scott Road house.
I should have kept that couch.
Saul's a famous historian now
and David's an even more famous medical scientist.
I have a smaller second-hand couch these days,
covered in white bull denim, it cost R20
from Barkhoff's up the road from that house
and it's served me well, but Cyrus Vance wouldn't have
                                            fitted on it.

He was a big man in a suit, of course,
and there must have been other big men with him
that day but I can't remember where they all fitted
in my semi-detached lounge, perhaps they stood
                                    behind the couch.
Who was he meeting there,
apart from my obvious friend,
and did we have coffee and biscuits
(the way the security police brought their own
custard slices with them when they arrived
to interrogate Welma in her flat)?
I was one of the crowd back then
as now, he wouldn't even have seen I was in the room,
in a corner, staring at my couch with him on it.
Even though it was my house.

What did he think of that scruffy street and the living room,
mould up the walls and Venda cloths covering the chairs?
A house built for nineteenth-century families who seldom ate
                                              meat or bathed.
And that strange trailing fern we had on the mantelpiece with
                                         its fat bundles of fronds
that lived another fifteen years after I left the house –
did its spores make him sneeze?

Later that year I had dinner at a long yellowwood table at
                                        Rozenhof Restaurant
where Robert McNamara held forth,
apparently here on some kind of peace mission
and all the recipients of Ford money sat dutifully
around the table looking at our plates,
thinking of napalm and Vietnamese palm trees
and children falling through his fingers
like the breadcrumbs falling away from our knives.

These men were like visitors from outer space
to us, but in fact we were their outer space,
aliens they were trying to steer into their holding pens.
They didn't even get indigestion.
They didn't even get dust on their shoes.
They talked and talked and talked even when they were
                                                 listening
and here we all are twenty years later,
just as they planned it.

AND ALL THE TIME

*Venice, 11 September 2001*

Venice came to fetch me at the station.

I was on my way from Tremosine to Refrontolo
via Santa Lucia, just a coffee
and a glimpse of platform life would have made me happy
but Venice came to fetch me
and said stay a few hours,
here's the Canale Grande to keep you safe
from melancholy, come,
walk down the steps,
even the American teenagers are doing it,
it's easy.

It was really Venice,
the whole movie set
smiling at me, hands outstretched.

Marco Polo. Serge Diaghilev. Joseph Brodsky. Me.

The movie where you fall in love
with the stranger in the piazza
and he looks back at you as he walks away
and his eyes say follow me –
and you become the woman
he wants to be followed by,
and the gondola waits for you
in the small canal framed by lamplit palace windows.

\*

At this distance,
                    at this remove,
      I recall stormy weather – the sunlit patches of it –

the grey dockside where hard-eyed young Hasidim were
                                      drinking tea,
and the closed faces of the walls around Campo del Ghetto –
          the storm reaching me as I got there,
shepherding me back along Rio Terà San Leonardo,
across the Canale di Cannaregio and through Lista di Spagna,
          with its blazing clouds and black showers
        showing me where to hurry

as I elbowed among the crowds
            and crowds of young Americans on every bridge,
                          at every intersection –

the sky's gold angel wings beating
over empty houses
                melting into rain behind me,
its thunderous murmur urging me toward shelter
as the light grew deeper,
hurrying across bridges past
                the dusk-pink waters of secret kisses,
      flashes of blonde piazzas where little churches
              hummed to themselves,
     men studied windows filled with costumes
               for a masked ball,
    a dog dozed against a barrow of maps,
   two women compared aubergines against the light

into a cathedral where young boys sent the silver shafts
                              of their voices
into the dark
           and an old lady knelt alone,
to wait

until the rain stopped, it was safe to run for the station

to sit near three Romany men making an espresso last
                the long damp hour before a train came
to take them somewhere else, or leave them behind

and the Americans buzzing and bartering at every corner
called each other to look at the pillars, the walls,
      the barges with their singing cargo,
           sent each other promises and addresses
across the choppy canals shining in the mottled stormlight
to meet later, to meet tomorrow.

                *


The sky cleared, there was time before nightfall
to step away
           onto an island of death, blindingly white
           and tidy, its graves and gravestones
           rigid as lacquered hair,
           its grass in uniform, its wreaths marking time
           in plastic and satin melodic precision –

only the miniature toys, the tractor the truck and the dinosaur
on a little boy's grave, toppled this way and that
in the wind, too light to lie still.

At this distance I wonder
where they were in the hour after I left,
the young Americans, when the message came,
and silence fell over them,
and they started to flee –

      \*


Venice let me leave without prophecies or warnings,
handing me back my eyes and tickets onward
                with an easy smile
and as I tried to scatter coins of thanks in my wake
waved them aside
               saying only,
     you're welcome here, it's no trouble
     to hold all of this open to you, it weighs nothing,
     you weigh nothing,

like mist you pass over my skin
and I am not here, this city is emptiness
in the shape of a dream, a dream's shell,
an old shell rolling in waters no one can enter.

      \*


                And all the time the world was changing
                     and there was no sign of it,
                        no turbulence in the canals,
            no sudden scattering of the birds and men.

                            My 9/11 was a day in a city
          with nothing better to do than cloak me lightly
                  in a thundercloud of antique beauty,

like all the future's ghosts
I was free to wander here,
watching heaven's storms gather and spill
and the small gold flares that catch the cobblestones
afterwards in the wet silence where clouds soften
and sunlight drips down its walls.

## Monument to the South African Republic

*(on some photographs by David Goldblatt)*

The long dry grass collects our history
and every few years burns it off
in a frenzy of memory.

Here it grows for two policemen who died
for the same cause, in Afrikaans and Zulu,
and who lie in heartfelt English
among broken cans and paper scraps
the grass has gathered for them,
for my lovely husband, from his lovely wife and children.

And here, around a modest stone obelisk,
memorial to the dead republic
erected on the day of its birth, the grass sways its long stalks
dried to the colour of biblical corn, sifting the summer wind
that brings grains of brick, cement,
old seeds and dog hairs to form a carpet
for the sparrows that visit, the tramps who sleep here –
for the town has understood to build
its street of chain stores and municipal offices
leading in the other direction, away from this
weathered, semi-literate scrap of older time.

In a graveyard a white concrete arch
loses its letters one by one leaving their grey shadows behind
like stains, vow of the dead soldiers
who came to rest here in a flag-shaped myth,
and the grass leaves a bare gravel patch
naked to the sun lest we forget, lest we forget
how nothing grows from such valour.

But just beyond the borderline of thirsty eucalyptus trees
it grows again, long and soft and ready to catch
someone's cigarette, some beer bottle splinter
smouldering there after a raucous night of farewells
and burn fast, and lay itself down as ash over the past.

# Eight frescoes from the lost palaces of Zanj

*the furious women bare themselves*

the furious women bare themselves
issuing a challenge no man should accept

to the troops invading the squatter camp
in buffels and ratels spiked with guns

smoke races from cooking fires and burning houses
the armoured vehicles have shuttered their windows

dare to look, dare to look
the naked women shout at the helmeted boys

who close their eyes as they advance
in the driving rain, rifles cocked and dripping

charcoal streaks erase the sky
iron walls buckle and the women's bodies shine like sweat,
                                                                        like steel

rain soaks the soldiers' shirts
the women feel the ash stroking their thighs, their bellies

smoke puffs erupt like kisses from the guns

*the four students run for the border*

the four students run for the border
with ochre footsteps remembering their land

from all sides blond hair thorns and blue spear thorns
                                          pierce their skin
and fear summons its shadows to track them

but they keep running bright-eyed,
thirsty as buck for the green clearing that must lie ahead

to the left the earth is cracking
tyre tracks slither forward hungrily

to the right mottled commandos leopard-crawl over the soft
                                                    new growth
crushing the water out of its skin

the four friends are almost at the end
their fingertips reach for the barbed wire fence

they are leaping,
all their bright blood is leaping

*he hides all night while they murder his family*

he hides all night while they murder his family

the shadow of a cold street
and the shadow of his body hunched like a fist in one corner

light of a window,
shadows moving like cries behind glass

how much you can hear when it's so dark

the lord is my shepherd I shall not want
my lamb is called Boo
what colour is that?
yellow!

such bright clear yellow
flame bright

the shadow of his body
is beating like a heart

like a shot, and another, and another

he holds himself
there is nothing but darkness here
his breath carries him through it like wind

no one can stop the wind, he lets himself go with it

*they were caught and chained in a van*

they were caught and chained in a van

they look lovingly out over the veld
as the van drives, drives and drives

laughter and memory pour from their eyes
through the bars, streaking the air with sunset
                            oranges and pinks

as the van drives through the bitter winter fields
swerving and braking, slamming their bodies against
                                  metal walls

a boy who taught hens to circle dance
a girl who cut bibles into true stories

this is their last journey and they are escaping
breath by breath onto the road, through the dry grass

towards the fields where the cosmos flowers every year
despite the drought, magenta and mauve armies, self-seeding

goodbye, they are calling to each telegraph pole,
goodbye, goodbye

*she gave birth while prison guards tortured her and laughed*

she gave birth while prison guards tortured her and laughed

only a goddess could do this,
and now without the sun's blazing chariot
or a cloak of thunder,
without spirits or eagles or rivers to command

she must be a goddess alone,
must leave her human heart somewhere helpless
and roar until she broke open

in a grey cell, bearing a daughter who would hate her
for the smell of laughing vultures that entered her at birth
and never left her

only a goddess could survive this
with clear eyes and a graceful back
sweeping the yard of her freedom without regret
unloved and magnificent

*a six-year-old boy is digging a grave for a baby*

a six-year-old boy is digging a grave for a baby

he finds a red marble
and a strange metal thing like a buckle, with sharp points

he watches an ant drag a crumb of apple flesh towards
                                              the grave
and digs a shallow trench to steer the ant in a safe direction

when the hole is as deep as his knees
he starts to make footholds in the walls
like a mountaineer's ascent path

russet leaves keep blowing into the grave
he presses them into the tops of the walls, a frieze

he makes a small cave in one wall, a storage chamber
for the marble, the buckle, and the other apple someone
                                              gave him

then he fetches the baby in its shroud,
places it in the grave and curls up next to it

he watches the ants as they make a path around the baby
taking crumbs of earth and leaves to the corner

where they're digging a tunnel

*the colours there*

the colours there

brown hands
white stones

green wind tumbling through green grass
blue water blue sky
and the grey veils of winter

tangled together across so many years
rope of cold longing

a prison rainbow

*like paper flowers unfolding in water*

like paper flowers unfolding in water

the artists swirl through halls and corridors,
releasing the shapes no one has named yet

of things once remembered and often dreamed

their arcs and spirals unleash every story
dissolving it in the unlocked light

of these crumbled palaces
gone ahead of the historian's pencil

vanishing into the archives of passing raindrops

until only pale shadows are left
that spill onto fingertips touching the stones

a faint sparkle

that could be dust of ancient seeds, or gold, or words

## Man series I

Man holding a puppy.

Man stumbling back and forth
across the traffic lanes, spittle trailing
from the corners of his mouth.

Man making omelettes at a deserted hotel
for two foreign women who work while they eat,
small fluffy omelettes to eat in the warm rain on the terrace.

Man getting out of bed to fetch an extra blanket
for the woman asleep next to him,
in case the winter air wakes her.

Man carrying a woman's cases through the rain
at midnight, from an airport terminal into a car,
swift and silent.

Man, behind previous man,
forcing himself forward with an umbrella
and a hand demanding a dollar.

Man in vagrant clothes
facing a woman's determined camera.

Man carrying a crying boy into a field.

Man following two women up a road
treading on their heels, and when they say
'please leave us alone'
crossing to the other side of the road

and keeping step with them, grinning.

Man, snow-covered, arriving at the door
with a stack of birch logs in his arms
to feed his dying friend's stove.

Man overtaking on a blind rise
then forcing his way back into the queue
one car ahead.

Man clipping his toenails
in a first class carriage of the Frankfurt–Paris
                              InterCity Express.

Man laying his head on an older man's shoulder
while they watch the Senegal–Cameroon match
from the older man's sickbed.

Man walking naked into a room
where someone lies sleeping.

## The sad little poems

I like the sad little poems that poets write to themselves
when they're sitting at windows on hot nights
unable to write
anything worth calling a poem.
They're like drinks you buy yourself
in a bar on a rainy night when you're feeling homeless
                                             and subhuman,
you look at the guy next to you and know
he's also going to have the hardest time
getting through the night,
not even a dog would walk home with him,
you buy him a drink as well
and neither of you starts a conversation.

Sad little poems with no dog to walk home.
And I thank the editors
who leave them in the collections,
even though they have nothing to say
to the readers out there
who want something more fragrant,
with a recognisable main character.

## Pasternak's shadow

The chapter recounts how Stalin phoned Pasternak
to ask who Mandelstam was, if he was a 'master' –
and explains what Pasternak surely knew at once,
that Stalin was asking whether and what he would lose
if he followed his first instinct: to kill the poet.
Yes, Pasternak told him, Mandelstam is a master,
and saved the poet's life
for the endlessness of an exile
and the whisper of a prison death.

What made Stalin feel threatened
by this small man's unwritten poem?
the chapter goes on to ask and struggles to answer,
but I've stayed behind
in the room where Pasternak looks at the telephone,
I can see how his hand is shaking
as he breathes in what he's just done.

Of course Mandelstam is a master
and if he, Pasternak, with one clear syllable uttered in a daze
has saved the poet's life for the time it takes
a small boy to swoop past him on his toboggan,
his red face brighter than the sun of this unending winter,
he can live with himself another day
inside Stalin's cold protective shadow.

But the question that rises up
like the shadow of that shadow
will not leave him now,
it clings to his soul like a forest leech:
if it had been another poet,

if it had been the man three streets away
who shows him his dull rhymes about birches and soldiers
or the woman whose love poems
have been clogging his letterbox for years,
if it had been the professor who writes stale odes
in praise of nothing living,
would he have called each one 'master'
for the sake of their lives?

Would he stand up inside the mask of his freedom
and burn his own fine-tuned tongue
to keep one of them warm?
He wants to tear the telephone loose from its wall
so that there can be no more –
but he dare not – what if Stalin has Akhmatova's name
scrawled on a pad in front of him,
with a question mark?

## Love songs for Lake Como

*1*

The lake is learning blueness from the sky.
It's spring: trees at its edges urge it on,
already far into their green thirst.

Slowly the water lightens but there's black below,
and a silver shadow folding each bright ripple in –
the deepness and the memory of the lake

it clings to, for the sky is far away
and blue without conversation. The trees say nothing,
blue is their dream of sweet fruit

but in the end it is the lake's life at stake here,
its loneliness and its future.

*2*

The clouds and the mist and the snow
won't let go of this silver place
as spring comes with its green paintbox,
its almond brushstrokes up and down the black branches.

Through every cleft they can find in the hills
the clouds wind their wistful scarves.
Shawls of mist drift to the water's edge
leaving their taste on the cypresses,
swallowing the boat engine's heat
before it can warm the lake's skin.

High on the peaks snow stitches its last lace to the stone
like an exiled woman climbing, turning back
to throw her memories over the lost land

as if they could freeze there and wait for her,
turning to crystals, turning to lake light.

# Over there

*Berlin, November 1989*

Once I was in a city that held me back
until the last moment

so I walked its autumn hours, waiting,
walked a small trail through streets
with their faces turned to the wall,
their memories packed for flight,
their passports withering

but the city said, sit here, wait with me,
it can't be much longer,
something is brewing, hatching, ticking,
it can't go on like this, I can't.

\*

The underground is at the end of its years
in the east,
in the west, too.

The red velvet *kaffeehaus* chairs are worn through,
the patrons are worn down with coffee and cigarettes
and the children they had when already somewhat mature,
slumped over wrinkled copies of *taz* at the pre-war wooden
                                                        tables,
drinking their bowls of milky chocolate and thimbles
                                    of espresso
while their little anarchist heirs wail and wander around,
throwing fragments of television nursery rhymes at strangers

as if hoping for some entertainment in return,
something new from the invisible wonderland
*da drüben*, they're confused
about where it is, the one they belong to.

At this time the patrons correctly have nothing to say
to the packs of journalists stalking the quarter
where yesterday's enemies face off
through the blank stares of their young men
held on the leash in the police vans idling in side streets:
the bullets are still real, still as real as the blood,
that's what keeps everyone strung tight like violin wire
on a treasured instrument that just won't sing,
as if the air's too hard or the sky too bare.

The patrons have earned their clairvoyance
with years and years of graffiti and underground news
and the hunger of those who stay loyal to the old forests
while new agro-economies are flourishing
on the faraway steppes and the prairies.

They can tell you how it will end for them, for you,
on the other side and the other other side,
they won't be the first to run laughing across the border
the wrong way, making it disappear with their own bodies,
they don't really want to see the other half
of the city that will blame them for being here and for
                                                       not being
more shiny than this, for not being New York or Frankfurt
or anywhere in California.

And there, on that side,
the underground has ground to a halt just before the border,

the last roll of tickets hangs limply from the machine,
the platforms stand still, as bare as an empty sanatorium
when all the patients have been released
healthy again, ready to fill the streets with their happy
                                            intentions.

Only one soldier patrols slowly
up and down, up and down,
letting the sound of his boots on the bare cement
hypnotise him for the last time
in this quiet grey dream
they've already started chipping at just two blocks away:

the full city is coming to fetch the empty city,
from both sides the noise is growing,
the cars, the hands reaching out,
the welcome money and the bananas,
and the children wailing in the old red *kaffeehaus*.

History wants to
get its hands on this city
all over again.

                \*


The great thing about a wall
is that it means what it says.

So when it comes down
there's no doubt about it:
something phenomenological is different,
something material has changed.

And the great thing about a balloon
being wound and knotted into the long pink shape
of a dachshund at ten-to-nine on a Thursday night
in a cabaret circus club full of smoke and wine
is that it proves how serious grown-ups are about playing.

So that when someone stops
winding an orange balloon into the shape of a rabbit
and cries out 'listen to the radio! the wall is down!'
you know this is completely serious
and could only happen in a cabaret
about history in a city with no country to keep it warm.

And the great thing about Potsdamer Straße
in November 1989 is how cold it was,
poor-migrants-selling-their-old-clothes-cold,
Baltic-Caspian-Black-Sea-Siberian-wind-cold
up and down the wide barren pavements,
and the thrift shops offering black flannel nightshirts
worn thin but with their rich colour unfaded,
black polo necks of the thinnest nylon,
black trilbies for small-headed men,
fifty pfennig each, cheap warmth for a solitary foreigner
waiting for the city to say, it's over, you can go now.

So that sitting in a café with a bowl of hot chocolate
held in both hands seemed like the warmest softest place
                                                      on earth
and the black clothes shone against the grey cement of winter
like a forest still intact.

And walking in a slow million-person circle
around the wall with its tiny perforations,

its teenagers with their fathers' hammers straddling the top,
its helmet-headed men sheltering their machine guns
from the crowd, the laughing million-person *Wessi* crowd
draped with the shawls of television lights
leaning in closer and closer to feel
the heartbeat of history changing its rhythm

you could imagine how cold it was on the other side,
and reach across, and blow clouds of your warm Western
                                                      breath
right onto the walls of the old monuments.

       \*


I stayed through that first weekend
when the city swelled and burst,
festering with desire and joy.

The underground trains burned out,
the first *Ossi* fists were raised against the Turkish migrants
                                                in the West,
the KaDeWe refused to donate its thousand brands of butter
or its in-store lavatories
to the wide-eyed brothers and sisters discovering
the nature of capitalist consumption,
its riches and its punishments.

By the next Monday everyone was sitting staring
                                          at the ground,
wondering where they lived now,
and who it belonged to

and I left, carrying a walled city in my left eye
and an unwalled city in my right,
my own before-and-after synapses of history

up Oranienburger Straße, back through Schöneberg,
across the bare patch of rubble where they filmed
                    *Wings of Desire*,
my black-and-white city with its orange rabbit balloon
never to be knotted by the young magician
fading behind me,

each of us pulling our old overcoats tighter,
walking in thin shoes our separate ways.

# I SAW YOU COMING TOWARDS ME

*(Praise poem)*

I saw you coming towards me
from far away.

From far away
I recognised you.

I meditate on why your appearance is that of a good man.
Bear. No. Faithful St Bernard, gentle rescuer.
Are you coming to drag me to safety, to shelter me.

Your domed head, your shield of shoulders, arms –
symmetry of a father's boulder love.

Bare skull unafraid of the sky's temper.

They say you're a poor man, a man of the poor,
your hands have made your soul breathe.

St Bernard's steady gaze, stern with love.
No. Bear. Flint-eyed. Now I see
the grey glints there, they come from stone.
Dead stone splintering, flash of false fire.

*I meditate on what you have gathered to you and thrown aside
in the course of your life*

Man walking towards me through valleys
that throw their shadows over you.
As you walk you grow bigger – are these your wives
                                    and daughters
spreading shadows around you.
Are these your lands and cattle, your brothers and sons.
Your eyes are the valley's wells, deepening as your smile
                                              spreads.

You are huge now you are a leader of people,
your shadow spreads wide like the rainclouds we pray for
that build and build until their grey swollen thunder-laden
                                                hearts
burst upon us hail batters us water floods over us
we lose our footing we must swim now
where the rain takes us our houses are broken planks
                                    swimming behind us
and in the wet light of evening we see you have gone,
you have vanished into the place of secrets.

And you return, you return from that wilderness of treachery
                                                and thorns
where you fought your war which now you bring back
                                      to lay at our feet.
They say life was terrible there, they say you were the one
                                                to fear,
commander of kindness and torment. Your body is hard
like a drum beaten in victory.

Now you have found sunlight and a suited street to walk in,
where did you leave your valley promises.
Your body is rounded and full, did you eat them, did you
                                                          sell them.
Your dance is slow and deliberate, the street settles under it.

From your eyes I see that you own only this one suit
but you are glad of gifts, you wear them as if they were yours.

*I meditate on the beauty of distant danger*

Man of whirling scythes and knives,
feet in the soil, eyes caressing an army of young warriors

with whips and jungle pits
teaching them to turn their whimpering nightmares

into roars that can kill even the smallest creature,
make them cry in pain, show them

what it takes to break an enemy's spirit
and make him love you.

*I meditate on my own small imagination*

Kindness is all I can imagine, my weak arms know nothing
of the power I see rippling in you.
I can't find my way through your heart,

doubts like a cloud of bees cover my face and I try to fold
                                                          inward,
to become tasteless as stone, safe from my doubts and
                                                        from you

coming too close, if your hand touches me
the pressure of your generous hand increases on me

– is this kindness? can I return your grasp?
I try to run into a cave of safety.

How beautiful your shadow is
spread across the mouth of my cave

still, still I want to see someone kind and strong
who will be on my side coming towards me

when you come looking for me
my cave shrinks, my dream of kindness
seems like embers of an old myth,
ash in my mouth.

*I meditate on tragic riddles*

A good man gets caught in a trap by evil forces that
                                        bring him down.
What's new?

Parsing the sentence:
how good?
was he caught or did he look for it?
was it a trap or a good idea?
how evil?
forces beyond one man's power to resist?
did the evil forces bring him down or was it
something else – like good forces?
can a good man be brought down by good forces?
is he down or just floating between mountain peaks?

*I meditate on how you're just like all the others*

Versions of you

all collapse around that sentence:
He offered to massage her.

Every woman knows that moment
when honour throws off its cloak
and starts to take, take what it wants.

He offered to massage her.
He said: You must be cold, here let me –
He said: I just want to –
He said: You're so tense –
He said: Here baby –

Every woman knows that moment.

*I meditate on sand beneath the sea*

Where the tide has pulled back the sand is filthy
or so it seems, a grey-brown colour like polluted mud
streaked with crushed things that barely glint with grains
                                        of mineral life.
Hours from now the water will return and what lies there
                                        will sparkle
like a land of emeralds and pearls. It's only the undrinkable
                                        water
that makes it shine like this, trickster sea, laughing at
                                        our thirst
with its delicious shimmer.

I'm just one of the dry shells under your feet,
so small you wouldn't notice me, maybe you'd grab at me
to pick your teeth absently as you walk along,
singing your ringtone song,
smiling at the boys who recognise you and call out your name.

I wish I were even smaller.
I don't want to be seen, touched, smiled upon
by you, coming towards me.

*I meditate on dreams come true*

He stands adored and steady
as a stone on a high mountain,
nothing holding him back from falling on us all.
Men cheer. Women cheer.

All the street lights bend their sodium crowns to greet him.
All the ragged boys acclaim his polished skin.

He is the son and father of their past,
he sings the songs they dreamed
would bring the stolen cattle home
and dances with the slow beat of a chief's heart

singing his way to the car with the tinted windows,
surrounded by warriors in black suits
and hidden eyes, spilling his song along the road
like cattle vanishing into the distant hills,
leaving oil streaks on the tar and a smell of burning tyres.

*I meditate on the power of art*

Make him a cloak of metaphors
stitched from the velvet napes of many cattle.
Praise him.
Create him anew.
Save him for history as he shrinks inside his suit.

*Coda Praise song for a man coming towards me*

Once you came towards us bravely as rushing river water.
You flowed thunderously and sweetly towards us with your
                                        understanding.

Now you trickle through that same river bed
like the thinnest trail of spittle left by a sick man,
your roar clatters like pebbles thrown by boys into dry gutters.

Your breath sets fire to the frail crops.
Your feet stamp the floor of the house until it breaks open.

You whose blood is as dark as the blood of a lion
when it has been poisoned by honey from the hives of a nation,
eaten and spilled wide across the floors of so many houses –

on your way home you renounce the peacock's feathers,
                                    mocking them
and take for yourself the leopard's pelt as if it was your own.
See there where the peacock comes to meet you at your front
                                                        door,
he will walk ahead of you to sing your coming,
you wear him alive and whole
and the leopard's corpse rots in the hearth,
in your mother's hearth it rots.

Man who, when you come among us
makes our bodies seem to grow fat
and our clothes shine in your hot shadow,
but when you leave we see we are as thin as worn shafts
and our shirts have shrivelled to muddy rags.

Your legs had the strength of tree trunks when you strode
                                                       towards us
but now they are shrivelled, you are a man walking on old
                                           canes chewed by rats.

Man of three legs standing astride our land like the feast pot
you make us believe can kill hunger while you rise over us
but you eat your food yourself, your shadow fattens
while we watch with wide mouths.

You, landlord of the dreams of people,
hunter of our hopes who captures them
like an old bear that can no longer eat,
eagle with the ragged beak of a vulture –
beware the winter hour when your wings fail you,
beware the hungry boys with stones waiting
in the street where you will land, where you will wander
                                                         whimpering
among the piles of refuse left by your armies.

I saw you coming towards me
from far away.

From far away
I recognised you.

## Elaine's Garden

*1*

You lived in a dry place and watered it carefully.

I always brought flowers
to thank you,
to wish you happiness.

Nothing else seemed light enough.
Flowers expect to be thrown away,
no sin, no shame.

To know another person is not mysterious.
But to touch her is forbidden.

*2*

I look up now and then and
there you are,
half-turned from the kitchen towards the lounge,
mug of tea in your hand.

there you are,
walking in your slow way between the girls' room and yours,
something on your mind that you won't utter.

there you are,
in the yard, moving between the washing lines and the back
                                                    fence,
checking on something, fetching in the dry sheets.

That's all you do
and you keep doing it,
I'm keeping you there.

3

What to do when a person dies
who never told you her secrets:
paint her as she walked towards you,
smiling as she wanted you to see her smile.

4

Scattered around the city
your daughters and their daughters cry for you,
remembering that you said you were tired,
tired of it all, the girls with their babies,
the clothing accounts, the stray boys at the fence,
your body, demanding a kind of care
you didn't have to give.

You knew it would just go on.
They watched you turning away,
moving more slowly,
couch to sun porch,
porch to corner chair,
chair to bedroom
to lie down
just for a while.

5

In every house
there's a woman like you,
standing the way you do, at an angle to the room,
keeping it steady without seeming to,
pillar, brace, stay,
wearing old cotton, vigilant,
walking slowly from room to room
resting only the way the walls of a house rest.

Around you young women and small boys dart and flutter
or come to cling to your shadow for a moment.

You say no, and the fluttering young women run off
shouting yes, but come back bruised and crying.
The young boys fall asleep in your lap.

Winter by winter a blanket of permanence spreads from
                                            your eyes
through the house, the rooms fold themselves around each
                                            Sunday lunch.

Your summers are warm doorways where you sit,
smoking a cigarette,
watching the street beckon your children.

6

You've chosen a quiet vanishing,
letting first speech, then sight, then touch
leave the room,
letting the soft conversations of neighbours and friends
wash your cold skin.

By the time I come you're spending the heartbeats
of your last slow day of breath.
I stand in your doorway, then leave.

This time I've brought armloads of jasmine and buddleia from
                                          my spring garden,
knowing their scent is too heavy for your daughters
crowded together making sandwiches for a vigil,
letting the flowers scatter and drown in their buckets of water,

letting me pass through, as you always did,
turning gently away.

7

The young ones have no language for what's happening
and hold their own breath,
saving it for the wild howl they need
when you leave at last,
leave your own bed, deathbed, warm bed
of your dead body close to everyone –

these lost girls in their black sandals,
finding their faces suddenly grave and stiff,
walking in a prayer-spattered circle
around the open coffin full of you,
walking in a wobbling line out into the icy sunshine

and you not there to call them
back across the street, back home.

*8*

The house stands trembling
like a dream emptied of its voice.

When will the roof fall,
how long can it hold its breath?

Your girls dance around inside like butterflies,
hovering against the windows
they used to dream of breaking,

the open windows they won't fly out of,
beating themselves instead against the glass
where your fingerprints still touch them.

Here is a basket of ironing,
here is a baby boy,
here is a group of young women
turning magazine pages.

*9*

People whose daily presence never changes
are the hardest ones to lose,

as if the earth has tilted
and you keep falling away from it.

*10*

I say, I want to plant something outside the front door
that spreads and flowers, in memory of you.
Your brother says, no one will take care of it,
they're not interested.

He's probably right.
But I want that garden for you
that you would have refused,
I want you to come out here
and stand next to me and smile at what grows here,
its perfumed colours spilling over you.

*11*

Dear Elaine
this is all (I can say),
this is all.

## Tango for person and city

*Buenos Aires, July 2007*

*Abrazo*

If this is a tango
it is slow and warm
for an afternoon, pushing the windows open
onto familiar weeping pepper trees and traffic streams
then cold, spinning from one corner to another
of the wind.

*Salida*

The air falls in drifts
around us like clear snow:
this is the freeze and glide tango of winter.

And there are nut-brown rats
scampering around the crumbling *grandes maisons,*

no fear, no harm, they vanish
fleet-footed among the crusts of old stucco –

fleeting, a word for you, this first encounter –
where are you?

What brushes against my hand
is only my own jacket, half-open.

*Amagues*

The man in his black wool coat and brown cigar
leaning against his black car
in the tiny street outside a brass-edged door
that could lead to a private bank,
a primary school,
a police intelligence bureau,
a perfect brothel,
the tired apartment of his dying mother,
turns his face away as I pass.

*Volcadas*

Hibiscus pink and pretty is the Casa Rosada,
and cornice-laden in the style of buildings
where the corridors are darkest.

Today the only mothers on the Plaza de Mayo
are foreign, shepherding their scrappy children
across the grass between statues, plaques
and stone-faced pigeons.

An army of radio masts observes them
from surrounding rooftops.

The friendliest things are
the poles at traffic lights and bus shelters
you can lean against, trying to refold
your map in the wind.

*Baldoso*

These were once the municipal food halls.
Today linen shirts and silver dinner bells
spill across the market tables,
basted by trays of monogrammed cutlery
and pop art sunglasses, and a giant Duracell bunny.

Hacienda curtains float like harlot ghosts in the draughty
                                                                        aisles
between beef aprons and meadows of clay buttons.

For me silk panels
fall from a rail,
crocus petals of a swirling skirt,
scarlet, tangerine, lavender veils.

Children running on rude feet
carve trails of rattling cups and saucers
along the weary floors.

*Caricias*

Little leftwing spinach pies
laced with nutmeg cheese
are so fragrant on paper plates

and a cloud of questions floats
over the cups of maté –
are you Zulu?
do South African workers have unions?

The kindness of foreign comrades
is a sweetness all of its own.

*Caminando*

The last men of the day
manoeuvre the last deliveries
through lukewarm doors.

At the corners black bags pile and settle
spilling food only half-soiled,
shredded paper, metal bones,
thin rivulets of liquid that shine
blond, then red
in the late light.

Two bodies lay themselves down in an entrance way
and cover each other with newspapers,
becoming this night's warm replicas of the heroes
standing in grey alcoves nearby –
they are my landmark on endless Independencia,
the sign that this is the place to turn
for the street where my bed is tonight,
Las Piedras, Street of Stones.

*Golpecitos*

Above the counter the menu speaks
International McDonald's
modestly, not pointing out
that this is the inner core of the global nuclear reaction
we know as forest-stripping-climate-change-inducing-
dollar-parity-setting-McDonald's-burger-
beef-production, Argentina.

At eye level there are trays
of fresh breakfast pastries
with tastes and shapes unnameable
north of the Amazon basin.

I don't speak Spanish,
the waitron doesn't speak English.
I'm trying to buy a second cup of coffee.
She's trying to tell me I get a free refill.
Words and smiles fluttering helplessly
over the empty mug.

I give up and return to my table.
Her colleague appears at my elbow
with a full pot, freshly made.
All is clear, all is kind.

Two bag ladies with separate mouthfuls of muttering
leave holding paper cup refills,
the rumpled pacing man in half a uniform
gets a fresh pastry
and returns to his up and downing the narrow aisle,
frowning and chewing.
Safe here on this Sunday-lonely morning
we all are.

*Cadencias*

And there's your tango, in the tourist street,
man with a life-size cloth doll lady
that makes no effort to look real,
staring the laughing tourists down
with a tango designed to show them
something unkind about life,
about streets full of dancing couples.

*Molinete*

But your true home, the Café Tortoni,
is beautiful still in its *beaux arts* glow
and the gentle waiter in his professional soul
laughs at our mistrust, remembers everything we ask for,
smiles at the guest who wants
artichoke salad and hot chocolate,
makes the room seem as though it belongs to him, to us,
to any vagrant guests who have lived elsewhere
as he lives here.

*Cruzada*

When the bosses ran north carrying
all the dollars in the bank,
the Chilavert print shop workers took ownership
of the plant and its elegant books and nervous clients
not without struggle, but in the end
here they are at midnight performing their triumph
among the sleeping machines, it's freezing,
the factory floor erupts in song and
turns silent as the play introduces a virgin bride
in a white gown, like a ghost her tears grow flames

as she becomes pure rage, the walls glimmer
with holograms of all the gods and elders
who enchain her, they transmute by unknown power
into dancing prisoners and labourers
and will it work? will it work?

The audience applauds, throws coins and notes
into the basket passing down the rows, hugs all the actors
and heads for the empty street to hunt for taxis,
it's really cold out here.

Hours later, huddled under a borrowed blanket,
so glad to have reached this bed at last,
to be indoors, even wide awake
and shivering from a cold water bath,
I offer thanks to the resident cat
padding delicately across my suitcase.

*Resolución*

I can't say you held me close,
it was the first time.

One afternoon you put your arm around me,
the next day it was the narrow street again,
buses brushing my shoulders aside.

There was no promise
to meet again.

## Deer on the Freeway

Driving on the freeway near midnight
I saw a young deer stand suddenly on the verge
and step forward into my lane,
as if this was Norway, as if I was walking
in a winter story in the nineteenth century.

At 80 km/h you must keep going if you can,
swerve only slightly,
hold your lights steady.
The deer was still, alert, not yet alarmed.

Others saw it.
For a moment a spirit of carefulness spread among us,
four cars with four drivers moving separately towards the city,
each slowing like someone entering a forest of sleeping
                                        children,
awake in a new way, fearful of doing harm,
grateful for the care that others took.

Everyone knows what it means,
a young deer appearing in a city
unafraid, quietly standing on the road
as cars speed towards it.

## Phendukani Silwani

His name is Phendukani Silwani.

He was made of carbon and light
and has vanished forever.

*

Phendukani's voice, flying home from school
ahead of him one kilometre after another,
crossing the river, finding stone after stone in the cold water,
fetching his friend, his other friend, his dog
in from the hills to walk with him
through the bushes, one kilometre after another,

little boy on your way home –
'Where are you?' 'I'm here.' 'Where are you?'

*

His vanishing was efficient,
it barely scratched the air of the country.

His life endures forever
only here, where his footprints
sparkle in the river's memory.

*

Phendukani can write the alphabet and numbers.
He can tell a story on the classroom magic carpet,
he can kick a ball hard enough to hurt his foot but not the wall.

He hasn't grown into his knees yet.
In the ground they'll lie like scaffolding for an unbuilt tower.

In the classroom magic carpet there's a hole
each child falls through, remembering Phendukani,
falling into the mists of *Come unto me*,
following his voice with theirs
to weave a nest of hymns his spirit can fly home to.

*

Phendukani on a horse
panting through the beautiful valleys
to find a nurse, a doctor, a car,
turned back at the boundary
between the land and the highway.

Small saddlebag of life
slumped across the horse's patient back
nowhere to go but home
to the house that freedom has not blessed

hunched against his father's chest
holding his pain steady, borrowing the horse's breath
and his father's heartbeat to reach the last day of his life.

*

In the shadow of the broken house
those who love him stand together
to bury his burst body, shrouded
in death's cold exhausted air.

On the horizon the Ministers pause to wish them well.

> \*

When a child dies, who is responsible?
It's a complicated diagnosis.

When his liver turns against him,
who can say what story it has to tell,
what its tumours remember?

> \*

Let Phendukani Silwani stand for all Departments of Health,
all out-patient queues and closed wards and unbought drugs
                                        and spent doctors.

Let Phendukani Silwani stand for all Departments
                               of Education,
all unbuilt schools and untrained teachers and stolen food
                            and books bearing false witness.

Let Phendukani Silwani stand for all Departments of Housing,
all cracked walls and broken pipes and poisoned streets
                                   and lost gardens.

> \*

Phendukani is playing with an old tin and some wire.
And then he is not.

Phendukani is brushing his teeth.
And then he is not.

Phendukani is calling goodbye as he turns the corner.
And then he is not.

      *

Let Phendukani Silwani stand for all parents
with emptied arms and bent heads
whose tears hang like silver nooses in the air.

Let him stand for all children,
all parcels of carbon and light
who come only once, and vanish forever.

      *

Let Phendukani Silwani stand for himself only,
only he existed in his small body,
only he was there, looking out at us,
at the tall grass that hid him,
at the unreachable blue sky.

      *

Thank you for the paracetamol.
Thank you for the social grant.

## Poem for Which There Was No Title

Yes,
I've said yes
to you,
to going
as far as I must
with you.

\*

When I first saw you,
fabled visitor to our fabled land,
you were as real as a table or a chair
and it made perfect sense
that you were sitting there
with my name in your hands.

Over tea and *petits fours*
in the olive plush chairs
in front of the Pompeii mural

we had an entire conversation without a sound
while your minders mapped and folded
your coming days and nights.

By the time you left
we'd laid that journey to rest
and embarked on our own one
to be continued

(dangerously –
this that we'd started,
a dare thrown down
between our discreet shoes:
never show,
never tell,
never say
it wasn't real
enough).

By the time I left there
on my own I realised
I'd fallen down a well
and you were the one come to catch me
and keep falling with me.

\*

Old enough to know
this is worth risking everything for.
Old enough to know
what's done is done

and this is new,
this is the next spring
that comes and I could hope
it will be the last, the longest one.

\*

When you fetch me
remember to do it silently
so that no one will know

and when you bring me back
remember to do it without a word
so that I won't find out until long after.

*

Your hands, your stranger's hands –
watching them move
my wrists move,
my ribs open,

and then your eyes – they know
everything I know,
and what will come of it –

unsmilingly
you dare me to go further,
you promise nothing,

looking directly at me
you see the thing
I almost have a name for

flickering inside, catching, burning.

*

A thousand people have a claim on you
but you have a claim on me.

A hundred thousand queue outside your sleep
but you knock gently at my door

and yes, yes
I permit you to enter.

    \*

Everything was
preparation
for this.

All the tears and fevers,
all the cold cement survivals
are over.

Don't wait,
don't wait any longer.

    \*

Don't worry,
I've covered your tracks
though not my own.

Mine are wide open to all circling eyes,
filling up with eggs laid by the lady fly
who clung to the upright of my window frame
all of this hot fake summer winter's day
while her man rode her glossy back
and her wings shimmered,
shimmered and shimmered.

    \*

Not for me to ask,
do you remember?

Nowhere to walk
back to, together.
Not love of that kind.

What I touch
still bears your scent.
Love of that kind.

\*

Listening long enough
of course I'll find that you're only
my own dream made flesh,
that the solitude you breathe
is the one I've found
and we inhabit the same torn air,
separated by skin and oceans

each of us setting out
for the same impossible sky,
raising loneliness like a flag
on each memory we reach.

\*

This is a happy story.
Couldn't be otherwise,
given your life
and mine, given
but not taken.

Happy.
A story.
Long ago.
Far away.

## FROM FOLK DANCING FOR BEGINNERS

*He sets the tone*

In my country the president
rises
from a bed of red carnations

and then the children
sit down
each with a goldfish on their desk.

Their task is to teach it to
swim
better than it does already.

At the end of the year they'll
have to have to have to
show what it can do

and the president will
visit
with gifts of sandwiches and white flags.

*So where were you*

when I needed you?

I know, you were right here,
staring at me from the doorstep
saying get a grip, your needs are a joke

and of course you were right,
they were, I did.

Now you've come all the way in
and you're turning this way and that
in front of the mirror, offering me

a whole wardrobe of postures to record
breathlessly, and I'm trying not to yawn.

Show me something that makes me
want to dress up to match,
show me the germ of a good time, show me
something silkier than I can spin myself

and I'm all yours,
me and my fine adjectives,
all yours.

*The laws of physics are inviolable*

Now I realise
I just assumed
you'd be willing to share my lunch,
lend me your books, borrow mine.

Now I realise
you'd look at me and think
'you're of no interest'.

You'd never need a lift from me,
I'd never dream of asking you for one.

Parallel phone lines stretched
pole to pole along the national road.
Or an underpass and a flyover.
Both unending, and if I can look at you so nakedly
it's because not even my shadow exists in your world.
It's a plastic bag blown against a fence,
you pass it with your shades on, turning the volume up.

I wish I could tease you and pour you a drink,
I wish you'd laugh sometimes
and wonder what I'm thinking.

I can't keep scowling, it's bad for my heart
yet that's the only way I can stop you
flattening me with your clown-size mirror,
your nothing there but policy documents
bursting out of your pockets,
your voice like a jumbo all-the-trimmings hot dog.

*The coastline seems endless*

Everyone returns after a while.

The one you loved comes back
as a YouTube clip and you understand
why he left without you,

the one who loved you
comes back as the president
of a club your parents joined
at the time you ran away,

the one you were
wakes up one night
inside you

begging for mercy
in a voice you hoped
never to hear again.

But here they all are,
none of them looking at you
and all you can do is wait
for them to find you
ghosting their nights and days
and reach out, ready to try again.

*It goes like this*

First come the loud boys leaping sideways
thinner than my heart.

The girls say come, come, come
and the boys leap, and the wind blows,
its small kitten paws smacking the day
slightly skew and rosy.

They are throwing their arms around you.
Oh! how warm they feel!
They are throwing their arms around you.
Oh! be careful!

\*

The men in dark suits cross the stage in formation.
They are very tired.
They will have a drink standing up.
They will head for their cars without seeming to hurry.
There are hairbrushes somewhere, waiting for them.

\*

At the entrance to the country
the women beat drums
outside their front doors. They are so angry, their jerseys
stretch and snap in the wind.
Then they go inside without a word.

\*

Oh sad and skinny boys I can't get past you,
you're like fence staves across my road,
knobbly branches broken off and made to stand sentry
without a crossbar or knitted arteries of wire
to hold you steady, your bony smiles reassure no one.

You have ten ways to stave off hunger,
none of them good, and if I tried to hug you
you'd be shy and brutal in response, awkwardly
you'd stab me and run, and rightly so,
you have a gift for leaping through alleys to find shelter
from the wind that scours the last flesh
from your dreams, the wind in eyes like mine,
you fuck and smoke and sleep the hours into a brave
history around the thinness of your heart,
its eager smile, you know you could do something,
if it were only possible.

*You are here*

A bin
a concrete table
half a pigeon wing
a eucalyptus tree.

Standing at the edge of the gravel
I look into a valley.
It floats and folds like the cloak of a story.

Words wander through it
harvesting the air – rustling ants, furrowing worms,
just, just audible.

*

I put in petrol,
get the windscreen cleaned, give R5.

You overtake me wildly,
I hug the yellow safety lane.

Thank you, your hazards flash
and my brights flash, you're welcome.

*

Only here, only here
in an enormous country
love is a small and private thing
running freely between cars, across valleys,
up and down the Shoprite aisles

finding its missing parts in the wire bins
with the Special Offer crowns.

*Balancing*

How much does it weigh,
this ribbon of hours slipping into the sunburnt sea?

> *grains of air, splinters of blue water –*

The woman in the orange skirt – her hands like flying fish
laughing as they splash the sea over her hot shoulders,
how much, how little do they weigh?

> *we try to balance them, but how –*
> *on our own hands? on the light?*

And the toddler's screams of upside-down rage
                              in his sister's arms
to be put down, set free to wriggle into the jewel bed of shells,
do they weigh more than the mine shaft his father's father dug?

> *or count them, but it's like counting your own breaths,*
> *you get lost in the breathing of them,*
> *each one is the first –*

How much does the beach weigh,
relative to the hectare of houses queuing at one old standpipe?
How light is this single day spread out on a striped towel,
relative to three centuries flooded with loss?

Between and between, the taxi stands with its doors open,
its dusty mats glittering with the salt prints of feet
clambering in to fetch a sunhat, jumping out again.

> *and this is where we've got to,*
> *and this is where we are for now*

*Arīb is Known: Six Songs in Search of a Singer*

(2017)

*1*

Arīb is known
not at all

she lay down in her cotton shroud
to sleep where the souls of *mughanniyāt* sleep
in the whispered songs of the sand

        \*

Arīb is not, she is
not Rihanna
not Janis or Joan
not Billie or Edith
and yet

not Nina or Miriam
not Subbulakshmi

and yet
and yet

        \*

her voice is low-pitched honey-wound
says no one at all

the light in her songs is
pomegranate rose pistachio tangerine

say the miniature
windows of paper

so far down the tunnel
of folded tales

    *

is she a dragonfly
a curlew
a falcon
a phoenix

Arīb
Arīb
breath rippling on ancient waters
Arīb
Arīb

    *

Arīb is known
not at all

she lay down in her cotton shroud
and she sleeps where the souls of *mughanniyāt* sleep
in the songs lost to the sand

2

Arīb sings, how she sings
feelings learnt at her masters' feet
in palace rooms, in fountain light

messages from heart to heart
does she breathe them?
whose trembling passes through her?
does her voice sound like the touch of her hands,
like the scimitar tip tearing a veil,
like the laughter of silver on glass?

\*

impertinent questions,
cast like hooks down the centuries

it is said
that she loved, was loved
was owned, was traded
was spent and replenished
owned those who owned her
it is said

the biographer has the right to know
and to show only what Arīb showed
as she sang in the way that they say she sang

\*

unspecified her
hair colour
ankle curve
wrist turn
elbow arc
neck tilt
eye depth

mouth
mouth
mouth
mouth

most famous
most skilled
most brilliant
most passionate

inaudible
invisible

3

also naturally
daughter mother servant master mistress
wielder of praise and contrition
dazzling player of stroke and counter-stroke

angry tired playful desperate
exhausted glorious jealous frightened

huntress of love for love
for song for the tent of words
the arrows the hoofbeats the flight
for the jewelled glances gifted
the eyes traded for lips
the whispered lilt the fluttering curse

smiling that smile

\*

also just
one of the girls
the everywhere the gorgeous girls
starstrung across the night
of the great city
the lost city

singing softly
so far away so
silent

4

heart of her own
risk taker, deal maker,
famous eloper, sung of by poets and princes

secret bride of a caliph's servant,
unrepentant prisoner of salt and bread

heart capturer
caliph after caliph

diligent devotee
caliph after caliph

5

I come to you
in bad faith Arīb

believing that your fame
was no different from anyone's fame

that what you wrote and sang
was just a *qayna* thing,
a party trick or two repeated
by the next dazzling girl
with pearls in her throat
and diamond thoughts

*

a singer at a caliph's feet
whose honeyed amber tongue
can bind the soul
in chains as sweet
as muskwood oil
an ancient trope

and here it is
in flesh and blood

heated
cooled
by centuries
a desiccated legend
leaving small secrets
fallen into stone
like fossil eggs

6

Arīb
slips in and out of view
craft on the ocean
gull in the storm

swoops, soars,
tumbles

washes up
in our indices

\*

is not, we know,
Sotiria, hollow-eyed with loneliness
or Patti, faithful to the dream

or is, is

slipping in and out of view
and so
let's start again
Arīb,
reaching toward you through your shadow
through the never vanished, never captured
strands of perfumed air
calling out to you
return, return

from *The Loving and Lovable City (May Not Yet Be Here):*
*An Atlas of the Cape Peninsula*

(2023)

# Songs for the tourist in Cape Town

## Booked tour

In the sleek bus
you settle, this generously moulded seat is yours
for the day, you'll travel at ease with your bones
through several landscapes undisturbed

by the dusty indifference of the air outside the windows
and pour like champagne into the wide-rimmed welcomes
of selected restaurants along the route,
where the staff will be genuinely thrilled
to have you so close they can almost touch
your marvellous foreign world.

You think you're visiting our country
but in fact we're visiting yours
in all its cool perfection, its quiet certainty

that everywhere is penetrable in comfort,
gentle on the tongue, easy to swallow
and temperature-controlled to suit your skin's desire.

## ITINERARY

Shop.
Eat.
Drink.
Smoke.
Dance.
Swim.
Climb.
Find a pharmacy.
Sleep.
Dance.
Drink.
Smoke.
Stand on a pavement at dawn
waiting for an Uber.

## Gap year tourist

Little shell in the breeze
bouncing eagerly
from scene to scene
pretty as a postcard stamp

and each scene bounces you off
like a fly because you lack the key
that opens its door, you can only
lick a drop of sugar off the handle

before it snaps down and flicks you
back to the hollow room inside
that you long to fill with him

who never will find you, catch you, hold you
so take another tour,
strike up another conversation with a stranger.

## Departure

As you wait for the final call to board the plane
perhaps you'll reach back into the residue of your last night
trying to recover the feeling that slipped through you then –
how, when the heavy herded day was at an end

and stepping through the doorway you prepared
a simple face to join the dinner group
just at the threshold a small bush twitched
as if it housed a secret animal

and all you wanted was to kneel down there,
leaning your cheek against the cool wall
and listen to the bush and all it sheltered settling for the night.

Always we carry another self with us, not quite a shadow,
reaching beyond the outline of the day
towards the unnamed things that wait for us to join them.

## Once I travelled

Once I travelled with someone who knew the way
to where he was going.
At a certain point
I slipped off his map and onto my own.

That's how you change your nationality.
Each minute is a fork in the road.
Vodka or berries? Stars or salt water?
The coordinates of the grid hold steady: bathroom, bed, bus.

The weight of the suitcase draws your contours.
Curiosity and exhaustion calculate the scale of your steps.
The buildings stare down at you, waiting for your legend
                                                  to appear
and the taxi touts wave place names at you
in the language they think you speak.
The only thing you may not do is stay where you've arrived.

## Sites of interest

### *Factreton*

Factreton, I can't get you out of my mind.
Who knows you, who ever speaks your name?
You're the little brother of Kensington and Maitland,
always tagging along, wearing their cast-off shacks and gangs.
Their backyard. Their unresolved crises. Their *gat*.
You don't even have your own map.

But someone gave birth to you,
called you by this peculiar name.
And magnetically you drew in people,
you grew houses made of iron and wood on sand,
you spread warm gravel pavements in loops and squares
                                            around them.
You have a clinic. And a dancing school!
So at least once, someone put their arms around you.

And in a house on the corner of 8th Street and Lily Way
there's a family whose story stretches back to Yogyakarta.
The blood they spill on your sharp edges
sings ancient Indonesian songs.

## CLIFTON

Four flights of age-defiant steps lead down
to a thesaurus of perfections
that can't help being beautiful beyond reason:
four tidy scoops of bright blue consonants,
the occasional low moan of moonlit vowels
and a Lamborghini's worth of swimwear
in jewel drops on the crystal sand.

Part of the pleasure of contemplating Clifton
is tossing numbers into the brilliant air –
most expensive property per square metre,
most lavish marriage of space and views,
most outrageously priced parking bay.

But let's not mock.
There needs to be a gold standard
against which all the scruffier beaches can measure
                                        their dissonance,
their complicated relationships with rocks and tides.

## Brackenfell

There are places where nothing happens
and then everything happens.

Beige walls, dry grass, school uniforms,
race riot.

If all you had were these street names on a map
what could you make of them?
Only those who live here recognise its suburban soul,
dead space for anyone without a garage remote.
It offers nothing to the traveller passing through,
nowhere to stop for a coffee, a toilet,
a glimpse of unfamiliar birds.

And yet, memories of certain films and novels stir you to ask:
what mysteries do these tight flower beds and perpendicular
                              driveways conceal?

Probably nothing you haven't already encountered
in a family court or a shopping catalogue.

But then, race riot. And Brackenfell bursts open into history.

## ELFINDALE

Elfindale is a calm and gentle place
no one has heard of who doesn't live there.

Its fairytale name shields a past that's crumbled quietly
into the soil of careful lawns. Its families sleep with knowledge
of worse things that could have happened.
It seems legible to social scientists and estate agents.

How does one honour the life of such a place?
Where does its darkness go, its memory, its betrayals?
It was returned eventually to the dispossessed, they imagine
new housing developments, prime property values.

Small black hole in the city's universe,
it radiates almost nothing.
One of many lost to history's song and dance.
Only the soft-skinned animals on its grassy verges
wonder what comes next for them.

## Muizenberg

For all that the city sparkles in places and bleeds in others
it's these weathered corners that glow with indiscriminate joy.
So many mansions and tenements softening in the same
                                            salt air,
rust and mould leaning into each other,
old stone and worn plaster becoming kin.

Where the kids with surfboards don't hide in cars
from the kids with drugs and knives,
where the toasted cheeses and falafels and almond croissants
all sit on the same pavement tasting the sea,
where the communists and preachers and yoga teachers
are on the same WhatsApp group
and the rusted fences and bougainvilleas prick with the same
                                            force
there is a weathered place that loves its people.

And yes, there are rats and slumlords,
they own the same buildings,
but the people who live in them walk freely
along streets of windy sunlight.

## District Six c. 2020

Really, it's too exhausting to go through all this again.
They kicked people out of a cosmopolitan, richly viable
                                          neighbourhood.
Sent them off into the sandy wastes of the future.
Erected buildings there no one could call home.
Stepped around the brave churches and mosques that
                                            stayed put.
Left most of the plots of land to shed their tears into
                                            the wind.

Then gave it back in twenty-five years of tortuous
                                            negotiations.
One by one the removed people died of old age.
Now it's a happy cluster of conflicts
between owners and tenants, developers and heritage
                                            advocates
in the familiar urban way.
A post-liberation parcel of land.

Nothing much grows there except showpiece apartments
and small veld fires lit by the homeless with no land claim
                                            credentials.
And it has lost the halo of its tragic barrenness.

## THE CASTLE OF GOOD HOPE

Well, it has an unusual shape.
And whatever goes on there has been going on for a long time.
It's announced as the oldest building in the country,
if you discount all the other buildings that were destroyed
to justify its existence, soft and pliable homes
no match for the construction techniques of the gun.

Homeless Capetonians have claimed its outer edges
and honestly it would make a lot of sense
to give them the inside space as well,
at least as a piece of reclamation theatre.

But for now it squats like a giant's bootprint
among the cars and taxis and buses and jostling feet
moving past it with their backs turned.
Every few hours it swallows a party of tourists
but no one ever says if it was worth the cost of the excursion.

## Unmapped

how violence and sweetness live so close together
how cheap wine flows inside fine wine
how rage and laughter go indoors when the rain starts
how the street lamps break into dances at dusk
how there is always a full taxi standing still on the freeway
how the elephant trail is knotted with petrol stations
how moonlight slips like a fish between buildings
how sirens carve contrails in the air
how nail bars pulse on weekends
how tags fight wars of dispossession
how crates of whisky and beer fill the morning car park
how bundles of blankets move from street to street
how the mountains vibrate with inaudible abattoir screams
how exhausted loading zones wait for what will come next

how oil and water don't mix
how bleach and vinegar don't mix
how sand and eyes don't mix
how moonlight and sunlight don't mix
how yesterday and tomorrow don't mix
how the geometry of the geology paints the melanin rainbow

how new love climbs to the rooftop bars
how broken hearts hand themselves in at police stations
how squirrels and baboons share forests
how daisies creep down to the water's edge
how wheelchairs hide under bridges
how satellites follow our signals
how corners gather in shadows

how the trees lean northwest and southeast
how the moon slips away to the ocean
how the stars turn their backs on it all

how the leathered footprints of grey fur on tar
unspool thin red threads
that trace the route the soul took

## Source notes

'Causality and chance in love'
    'I remember the first time all of us heard children's voices in the quarry …' – Neville Alexander, prisoner on Robben Island, 1964–1974.

'I who live here, it is I'
    'This earth was the first to speak.
    I have been pronounced once and for all.' – Breyten Breytenbach, *Return to Paradise* (Faber & Faber, 1993, p. 75).

'Dispossessed words'
    The words in the poem come from research conducted for the Second Carnegie Inquiry into Poverty and Development in Southern Africa, 1984 (Southern Africa Labour and Development Research Unit, University of Cape Town).

'Walking songs for Africans abroad'
    'At the round earth's imagined corners' – John Donne, *Holy Sonnet 7*.

'Monument to the South African Republic'
(on some photographs by David Goldblatt)
    The photographs are:
    'Memorials to two policemen shot and killed here by robbers on 3 July 2002, Whipp Street, Memel, Free State. Three men were each given two life sentences for the murders, 24 August 2005';
    'Monument to the Republic of South Africa 31 May 1961, Cornelia, Free State, 24 August 2005';

'Memorial to two members of the African armed forces killed in what President PW Botha called the "Total Onslaught", Villiers, Free State, 24 August 2005'.

'Phendukani Silwani'
Nobuntu Mazeka is gratefully acknowledged for her detailed account of the conditions of Phendukani Silwani's life and death, which provided the source material for this poem.

'Arīb is Known: Six Songs in Search of a Singer'
Arīb'al-Ma'muniyya was one of the *qiyān*, the singing slave girls of Baghdad during the time of the Abbasid caliphate. Fuad Matthew Caswell's book *The Slave Girls of Baghdad: The Qiyān in the Early Abbasid Era* (I.B. Tauris, 2011) is the source of all the biographical details alluded to in this poem.

'Elfindale'
https://www.iol.co.za/capeargus/news/elfindale-familys-land-returned-84-years-after-they-were-dispossessed-of-it-453c9c9b-acc5-40e9-98d3-67e38cdadd32

www.ingramcontent.com/pod-product-compliance
Lightning Source LLC
Chambersburg PA
CBHW071002160426
43193CB00012B/1886